Snacks & Basic Side Dishes

TRADITIONAL KOREAN COOKING

by Noh Chin-hwa
Copyreader: Shirley A. Dorow

HOLLYM

Copyright © 1985
by Hollym Corporation; Publishers

All rights reserved
First published in 1985
Tenth printing, 1999
by Hollym International Corp.
18 Donald Place
Elizabeth, NJ 07208, U.S.A.
Phone: (908)353-1655   Fax: (908)353-0255
http://www.hollym.com

Published simultaneously in Korea
by Hollym Corporation; Publishers
13-13 Kwanchol-dong, Chongno-gu
Seoul 110-111, Korea
Phone: (02)735-7551~4   Fax: (02)730-5149
http://www.hollym.co.kr

ISBN: 0-930878-48-5
Library of Congress Catalog Card Number: 85-80452

Printed in Korea

CONTENTS

Author: Noh Chin-hwa

Copyreader: Shirley A. Dorow

About the Author

The author, Noh Chin-hwa, graduated from Seoul National University with a degree in Home Economics. Since her marriage she has put her natural talent in cooking as well as in flower arranging and painting to good use.

Applying her creative power to cooking she has contributed articles and pictures to women's magazines, and she used to give lectures at Home Economics' College and Women's Institutes. She also has introduced Korean cuisine, Chinese cooking and Western cooking through television, radio and magazines and has published several books including the Traditional Korean Cooking Series and Daily Card Menus.

Currently she leads an active life as head of the Munhwa Cooking School and representative director of the Korea Flower Arrangement Society.

About the Copyreader

The English-language copyreader for this cookbook, Shirley A. Dorow, has lived in Seoul, Korea since 1958 with her husband, Maynard W. Dorow, who is a missionary with the Lutheran church. They have four grown children.

During her more than 25 years in Korea Mrs. Dorow's hobby has been cooking with foods from the Korean markets. She has a collection of Korean food slides and has presented several Food Forum slide-talks for newcomers about western-style cooking using Korean market foods. She also wrote a food column for the Korea Times.

Mrs. Dorow is a graduate of Valparaiso University, Valparaiso, Indiana with a B.A. in sociology and religion and has licensure in early childhood education. She taught at Seoul Foreign School for 9½ years.

4

INTRODUCTION

This cookbook of Korean recipes in English has been prepared for the English reader with the hope that westerner cooks might experience truly authentic Korean dishes. Until now many Korean cookbooks have been presented in English, but they present only those recipes which westerners are presumed to prefer and they modify the recipes for western taste.

This cookbook is authentically Korean. It is a careful translation of recipes prepared by a woman who directs a Korean cooking school in Seoul, Korea for real Korean housewives who are actually using these recipes daily. Even the Korean style layout of the book is the same style as in Korean cookbooks and magazine cooking columns today.

It is true that these recipes stem from age-old Korean traditional recipes and as such are scintillating combinations of food and seasoning unique to the Korean heritage. It is also true, however, that Korean cooking is known for its individual touches. Each family has its own way of seasoning, and brides new to a certain family live with the mother-in-law, even today, long enough to learn these subtle nuances in cooking for their husbands.

The western reader, too, may wish to vary the ingredients according to individual taste. This is acceptable Korean-style cooking. However the recipes presented here present the current vogue based on years of refinement by the collective Korean palate.

Some of these recipes are presented in English for the first time. The step-by-step photo sequences make preparation quite easy and the glossary will help readers understand each individual ingredient and thereby develop a feel for the total impact intended in each recipe.

This book is presented in the hope that gourmet cooks interested in Oriental cookery may extend their repertoire of truly good food and enjoy authentic Korean cooking.

Seoul, Korea

Shirley A. Darow

PREPARATION TIPS

Korean food preparation methods are quite different from western ones. The main jobs in preparing a Korean meal are the cutting, slicing, seasoning and careful arranging of the food.

The cutting of foods before cooking is very important for appearance as well as convenience in eating with chopsticks. Slicing, chopping, scoring and sectioning the vegetables, fish and meat are techniques employed so that the food will cook quickly and be easier to eat. Also, each ingredient is cut or sliced into the same size or shape and the same thickness so that it cooks evenly and looks neat. Because of the quick cooking the nutritional value remains high as well. Scoring, which is the process of cutting slits in the meat, allows the marinade to penetrate further into meats and also prevents the cooked meat from curling up during cooking. Chopping the seasonings (such as garlic, green onion and ginger) allows for better distribution of the flavor throughout the dish.

Various seasoning sauces are used for marinating meat or fish before broiling or stir-frying. Other sauces are used on vegetables. The amounts of seasonings used may vary with one's preference and other ingredients may also be added to suit one's individual taste.

Some of the sauces are these:

1. Seasoning soy sauce: Combine 4 tbsp. soy sauce, 2 tbsp. sugar, 1 tbsp. rice wine, 1 tbsp. chopped green onion, 1 tbsp. chopped garlic, 1 tbsp. sesame oil, 1 tbsp. sesame salt (crushed sesame that has been toasted with a little salt added), and black pepper to taste. Pine nuts and extra rice wine are optional.

2. Sweet sauce: Combine 1 cup soy sauce, ½ lb. dark corn syrup, ⅓ cup sugar, ⅔ cup water, 1 tbsp. ginger juice or flat slices of fresh ginger, ¼ cup rice wine, 1 tsp. black pepper, and a little MSG in a pan and simmer on low heat until thick.

3. Vinegar-soy sauce: Combine 4 tbsp. soy sauce, 1 tsp. sugar, ½ tbsp. sesame salt, 2 tsp. vinegar, chopped green onion and garlic to taste.

4. Mustard-vinegar sauce: Slowly stir ½ cup boiling water into 7 tbsp. mustard powder; stir until a smooth paste forms in the bowl. Put the bowl containing the mustard paste upside down on a hot cooking pot (perhaps one where rice is cooking) and let it stand for 10-15 minutes. When the mustard is somewhat translucent add 1 tbsp. soy sauce, 3 tbsp. sugar, ½ cup vinegar and 1 tsp. salt and mix well.

5. Seasoned red pepper paste: Combine 2 tbsp. red pepper paste, 2 tbsp. soy sauce, 1 tbsp. chopped garlic, 2 tbsp. chopped green onion, 1 tbsp. sugar, 1 tbsp. sesame salt, and 2 tbsp. sesame oil in a pan and simmer on low heat until thick.

The final step in preparing most dishes is the careful arranging of the foods paying particular attention to alternating the natural colors of the foods to make a pleasant pattern. Foods are always arranged neatly in concentric circles, radial designs or parallel linear columns and never placed in a disorderly fashion. The dish must have eye appeal when presented for eating and recipes often give directions for the exact arrangement of the foods. The photos illustrate this important part of Korean cookery clearly as well.

The recipes in this book will generally serve 4-6 persons.

In the recipes in this book quantities are given in American standard cup and spoon measurements and metric measure for weight.

THE KOREAN DIET

For centuries the Koreans have eaten the fruits of the sea, the field and the mountain because these are the geographically significant features of the Korean peninsula.

The Yellow Sea and Sea of Japan offer excellent fish, seaweed and shellfish for the Korean table. The lowland fields produce excellent grains and vegetables while the uplands grow marvelous fruits and nuts—apple, pear, plum, chestnut, walnut, pine nut and persimmon to name a few. And the ever-present mountains offer wild and cultivated mushrooms, roots and greens. A temperate climate makes for four seasons with the fall harvest being the most abundant. Through the centuries the basic seasonings—red pepper, green onion, soy sauce, bean pastes, garlic, ginger, sesame, mustard, vinegar and wines—have been combined various ways to enhance the meats, fish, seafood and vegetables in the peculiarly spicy and delicious Korean manner. Various regions of Korea have special seasoning combinations—some hotter, some spicier—and each family also has its particular seasoning pattern. One family uses no salted shrimp juice in kimchi; another uses a great deal, but both claim kimchi as an integral part of their daily diet.

Kimchi is a kind of a spicy fermented pickle and accompanies every Korean meal. It is made from cabbage, turnip, cucumber or seasonable vegetables, seasoned with red pepper, garlic, onion, ginger, salt, oysters and soused salted fish juice, and fermented in an earthenware crock. Kimchi is made in large quantities in late autumn for use during the winter months. Autumn kimchi making is called kimjang which is one of Korea's most important household events. Kimchi contains good amounts of vitamin C and stimulates the appetite. Somehow, kimchi and rice make an excellent flavor and texture combination.

The basic diet includes at each meal steamed rice, hot soup, kimchis and a number of meat and/or vegetable side dishes with fruit as an after-meal refresher. In-season fresh vegetables are used at the peak of their season and dried or preserved for out-of-season use later on.

Korean table settings are classified into the 3-chop, the 5-chop, the 7-chop, the 9-chop and the 12-chop setting according to the number of side dishes served. The average family takes three or four side dishes along with rice, soup and kimchi for an everyday Korean meal.

When a family entertains guests for a special occasion, such as a wedding celebration or 60th birthday party, a dozen or more delightful dishes of different kinds are served according to the season. In addition, there is a characteristic way of setting the table for each occasion: New Year's Day Table, Moon-Festival Day Table, Baby's First Birthday Table, Ancestor-Memorial Day Table, Bride's Gift Table or Drinking Table.

Korean food is usually shared by diners. Each person has his own bowl of rice and soup, but other dishes are set on the table for all to reach. The main dishes and the side dishes are distinguished by the quantities served. At meal time, the smaller quantity of the food served will be one of the side dishes. Larger quantity dishes will be the main dish and nothing more will be needed except rice and kimchi.

As for the serving, all the food dishes except hot soups are set at one time on a low table that is set on the floor; at which one sits to eat. The main dishes and the side dishes which are shared by all are placed in the middle of the table. The rice and soup are placed in front of each diner. Chopsticks and spoons are used for eating.

In general the Korean diet is high in grains and vegetables which add much fiber to the diet, moderate but adequate in protein, both animal and vegetable (bean curd, bean sprouts, bean pastes, soy bean sauce), moderate in calories and low in fat and sugar. In short—a very healthy, well-balanced diet. It may be a bit high in salt if soy sauce is used heavily. It may or may not be red peppery hot; it is a matter of individual taste.

The Korean diet is changing and developing but basically the diet pattern has remained the same. Westerners may do well to examine this diet pattern and shift to a similar diet pattern for their own long and healthy life.

Egg Dishes
Bean Curd Dishes
Bean Cookery

Egg Soup
Talgyalt'ang (달걀탕)

Soft Bean Curd Soup
Sundubutchigae (순두부찌개)

Ingredients 2 eggs, ⅓ lb. beef, various seasoning, 2 dried brown, oak mushrooms, 2 small green onions, 5 cups water, 1 tbsp. nicely aged soy sauce, salt, black pepper, MSG

Method **1** Soak the dried mushrooms in water, remove the stems and cut them into thin strips.

1 Season the beef and dried mushroom strips.

2 Add the small green onion and beaten egg and stir slightly.

2 Cut the beef into thin strips. Season the beef and dried mushrooms.

3 Trim the small green onions and cut them into 2″ lengths.

4 Beat the eggs slightly.

5 Fry the beef and dried mushrooms in a soup pot. Add the water and bring to a boil. Add the small green onion and beaten egg

to the boiling broth stirring slightly. Check the seasoning and serve.

Hint Instead of stirring egg into the soup, place the bowl containing the seasoned beaten egg in boiling water and cook until set. Cut the cooked egg into bite-sized pieces and add it to the soup with the garland chrysanthemum leaves.

Soft Bean Curd Soup

Ingredients 3 cups soft bean curd, ½ cup clam meat, ¼ lb. pork, 1 green onion, 4 cloves garlic, soy sauce, 3 tbsp. red pepper powder, beef suet, black pepper, 1½ cup water

Method **1** Stir-fry the red pepper powder with oil in a pan to make the red pepper oil.

2 Cut the pork into thin strips. Trim the clams and remove the entrails.

3 Add the pork strips and garlic to the red pepper oil and fry together. Season with the soy sauce and add 1½ cup water.

4 When the #3 soup boils, add the soft bean curd. Bring to a boil again and add the clam meat and green onion cut diagonally.

Hint How to make soft bean curd: [Ingredients] 1 cup yellow soy beans soaked in water, 5 cups

Seasoned Fermented Soybean Soup
Ch'ŏnggukchangtchigae (청국장찌개)

1 Fry the red pepper powder with oil to make the red pepper oil.

2 Add the pork and garlic to the red pepper oil and fry.

3 When the #2 mixture boils, add the soft bean curd.

4 Add the clam meat and green onion slices.

water, 1 tbsp. brine for curdling [Method] Soak the beans overnight; rub with hands to remove loose skins; drain. Add 5 cups water, grind the beans in a blender and strain. Boil the strained bean liquid in a pot and let it cool to 180°F. Then add the curdling brine. An Epsom salts solution may be used as a curdling agent. Stir the liquid gently three or four times, so that it forms soft curds.

Ingredients   1 cake bean curd, ¼ lb. corbicula clams, 3 dried brown, oak mushrooms, ¼ lb. kimchi, 6-8 tbsp. seasoned fermented soybeans, ¼ lb. beef, 3 cups water, green onion, garlic, soy sauce, red pepper powder, MSG, red peppers, green peppers

Method   1 Cut the bean curd into large pieces. Slice the dried mushrooms, beef and kimchi into thin strips. Mix them with the green onion, garlic and soy sauce and stir-fry. Bring the water to a boil and dissolve the fermented soybeans in it.

2 When the soup boils hard, add the green onion, bean curd pieces and clam meat. Check the seasoning and bring to a boil again.

1 Mix the beef, dried mushroom and kimchi strips with the green onion, garlic and soy sauce and fry.

2 When the #1 mixture boils, dissolve the fermented soybeans in the boiling soup.

3 When the soup boils hard, add the green onion, bean curd pieces and clam meat.

11

Royal Soybean Paste Soup
Kungjungdoenjangtchigae (궁중된장찌개)

Ingredients ½ lb. minced beef, 1 clove garlic, sesame salt, 2 tbsp. chopped green onion, 1 tsp. sesame oil, black pepper, 12 gingko nuts, 4 skewers, ½ round onion, 3 dried brown, oak mushrooms, 1 green pepper, 1 red pepper, 2 tbsp. soybean paste, 1 green onion, ½ cake bean curd, sesame oil, MSG, ginger, 3 cups water

Method 1 Clean the round onion and dried mushrooms and cut them into thick strips.

2 Season the minced beef with the sesame salt, chopped garlic, green onion, sesame oil and black pepper. Shape the seasoned beef into square patties and broil them on a grill or in a fry pan. Cut the broiled patties into bite-sized pieces.

3 Mix the soybean paste, garlic, ginger and sesame oil, stir in 3 cups of water and bring to a boil.

4 When the mixture boils, add the sliced round onion, dried mushroom and beef patties.

5 Stir-fry the gingko nuts with salt in a fry pan, peel off the top-skins and skewer them on a toothpick.

6 Add the red pepper, green pepper and bean curd cut into square pieces to the boiling soup.

Hint Simmer this soybean paste soup on low heat in an unglazed earthenware bowl just before eating for its original taste.

1 Mix the soybean paste with the garlic, ginger and sesame oil, add the water and boil.

2 Shape the seasoned beef into square patties and broil them in a fry pan.

3 Add the sliced round onion, dried mushroom and beef patties to the boiling soup.

Bean Curd Casserole
Tubu Chŏn-gol (두부 전골)

1 Sprinkle the sliced bean curd with salt and fry.

2 Wrap the spinach firmly in a cabbage leaf and slice.

3 Place the seasoned beef and bean curd between the sliced bean curd, dip them into beaten egg and fry.

Ingredients A. 2 cakes bean curd B. ¼ lb. beef, ½ cake bean curd C. 2 cabbage leaves, spinach, various seasonings D. 1 round onion 2 oz. beef E. 2 eggs F. 2½ cup meat stock G. soy sauce, salt, black pepper, sesame salt, green onion, garlic, sesame oil H. flower-shaped carrot slices

Method 1 Slice the cakes of bean curd into pieces ¼" thick; sprinkle lightly with salt and fry.
2 Mince the B beef finely and squeeze the water from the bean curd. Mix the beef and bean curd with the seasoning. Shape the mixture into 15 meatballs ⅓" in diameter. Dip one side of the #1 bean curd piece into flour and put

the remaining meat mixture between the bean curd slices. Dip the stuffed bean curd pieces into beaten egg and fry until golden brown. Halve the bean curd "sandwiches".
3 Scald the cabbage leaves and spinach. Squeeze out the water and mix with the seasoning. Wrap the spinach firmly in a cabbage leaf and cut the roll into ¾" thick rings. Hard-boil the egg, peel it and cut it into a flowerlike shape.
4 Boil the D beef and slice it thinly. Mix the boiled beef and sliced round onion strips with the G seasoning. Layer this in the bottom of a shallow pan. Arrange all other ingredients, pour on the seasoned broth and bring to a boil.

4 Form the meatballs and skewer them.

5 Place all the ingredients in a shallow pan.

13

Mixed Vegetables with Egg
Okchayuk (옥자육)

Steamed Egg
Talgyal Yach'aetchim (달걀 야채찜)

Ingredients ¼ lb. beef, 1 round onion, ¼ carrot, ¼ bundle watercress, 2 dried brown, oak mushrooms, 2 Jew's ear mushrooms, 3 eggs, 1 tbsp. soy sauce, ½ tbsp. sesame oil, 1 tsp. sesame salt, 1 tsp. black pepper, 1 tsp. sugar, 1 tbsp. chopped green onion, 2 cloves garlic, MSG, 1 tsp. salt

Method **1** Slice the beef into thin strips with the grain of the meat.

2 Slice the round onion, carrot, and dried mushrooms into thin strips. Cut the watercress into 1¼" lengths.

3 Fry the beef and vegetable strips with the seasoning sauce in a fry pan. Top the fried food with three raw eggs and cover. After the eggs are soft-set, divide the cooked food into three equal parts and serve.

1 Slice the beef and vegetables into thin strips.

2 Fry the #1 mixture with the seasoning sauce.

3 Top with the raw eggs dividing the food into three equal parts.

Steamed Egg

Ingredients 4 eggs, 5 shrimp, 2 dried brown, oak mushrooms, ½ carrot, 1 tsp. parsley, 1 tsp. salt, 1 tsp. sugar, red pepper threads, 2 tbsp. tiny salted, soused shrimp juice, 4 tbsp. water, 1 tsp. sesame seed

Method **1** Remove the heads from the shrimp; scald the shrimp in boiling water. Then remove the shells leaving the tails intact.

2 Soak the dried mushrooms in water and clean. Squeeze out the water and cut them into thin strips. Cut the carrot into thin strips. Fry them in an oiled pan and season with the salt and sugar to taste.

3 Beat the eggs in an unglazed earthenware bowl or in a small

14

Wrapped Bean Curd
Tubussamtchim (두부쌈찜)

Ingredients 2 cakes bean curd, ½ lb. beef, ½ carrot, 1 round onion, 4 green peppers, 1 tbsp. chopped green onion, 1 tbsp. chopped garlic, ½ tbsp. sesame salt, ½ tbsp. sesame oil, ½ tbsp. sugar, 1 tbsp. salt, 1 egg, 5 cabbage leaves, 3 tbsp. flour, black pepper, MSG

Method **1** Wrap the bean curd in a cloth and squeeze out the water.

2 Season the minced beef with the soy sauce, garlic, chopped green onion, sesame salt, sugar, sesame oil, black pepper, and MSG and mix well.

3 Cut the carrot, round onion and green peppers into thin strips and fry them separately in an oiled pan salting each lightly.

4 Mix the **#1**, **#2**, **#3** ingredients and the egg with the seasonings.

5 Scald the cabbage leaves and dry off the moisture. Sprinkle the insides of the cabbage leaves with flour and then place the **#4** mixture on each leaf; roll it up as you would a jelly-roll.

6 Place the rolls on a damp cloth in a steamer and steam.

Hint You need to regulate the quantity of the water in the steamer and leave a 1¼″ space between the water and the food in order to steam the rolls well.

1 Mix the bean curd, minced beef, fried vegetables and an egg with the seasoning.

2 Place the **#1** mixture on each cabbage leaf and roll it firmly.

pot and season them with the sugar, water, salt and salted shrimp juice and stir well.

4 Add the dried mushroom, carrot strips and shrimp to the beaten egg and steam over medium heat for 20 minutes.

5 When half-steamed, top the mixture with the red pepper threads and chopped parsley.

6 Serve in the cooking bowl as is.

Hint **1** You may steam the bowl of egg mixture in a rice kettle, when you boil the rice, on top of the rice.

2 It is better to season the steamed egg with salt, not with soy sauce.

3 You may add minced beef instead of the shrimp or vegetables.

1 Fry the carrot and dried mushroom strips sprinkling them lightly with salt.

2 Beat the eggs well and season.

3 Add the carrot and dried mushroom strips to the beaten egg and steam for 20 minutes.

Stuffed Bean Curd
Tubusobagi (두부소박이)

Steamed Bean Curd
Tubusŏn (두부선)

Ingredients 2 cakes bean curd, ¼ lb. beef, 2 green onions, ½ carrot, 3 stone mushrooms, 5 dried brown, oak mushrooms, 1 egg, 3 quail eggs, ½ tbsp. salt, 1 tbsp. chopped green onion, 1 tbsp. chopped garlic, ½ tbsp. sesame salt, ½ tbsp. sesame oil, 1 tbsp. cornstarch powder, black pepper, MSG

Method **1** Cut the bean curd into pieces 1¼" thick by 1⅔" × 2" and sprinkle it with salt. Fry the sliced bean curd until golden brown on both sides. Make a D-shaped cut on the top of each piece, lifting out the top slice to replace later. Scoop out the inside.
2 Mince the beef finely and season it with the chopped green onion, garlic, sesame salt, sesame oil, black pepper, MSG and mix well. Soak the stone mushrooms and dried mushrooms in water, clean and cut them into thin strips.
3 Cut the green onions into thin strips. Cut the carrot into thin strips and chop finely. Hard-boil the quail eggs, peel and slice them in two or three equal parts.
4 Combine the minced beef, stone mushroom, dried mushroom, carrot, green onion strips and quail eggs with the sesame oil, sesame salt, black pepper, MSG, salt and starch powder to make the stuffing.
5 Stuff the bean curd with the above mixture. Dip the stuffed bean curd into cornstarch powder, then into beaten egg and replace the lid piece. Brown them lightly in a fry pan. Place the fried bean curd on a damp cloth in a steamer and steam 15 minutes. Halve the steamed pieces and serve.

1 Fry the bean curd pieces until golden brown on both sides.

3 Stuff the pieces with the stuffing and dip them into cornstarch powder.

2 Score one side of each piece into a "D" form to make the lid and scoop out the inside.

4 Steam the stuffed bean curd for 15 minutes and cut into halves.

Ingredients ⅔ lb. bean curd, ¼ lb. minced beef, 5 dried brown, oak mushrooms, 5 stone mushrooms, 1 egg, 1 tsp. pine nuts, red pepper threads, 2 tsp. salt, 1 tbsp. chopped green onion, ½ tbsp. chopped garlic, 1 tsp. sesame oil, black pepper, water, 1 tsp. sugar

Method **1** Mix the minced beef and mashed bean curd well with the seasoning and shape the mixture into a square patty.

2 Soak the stone mushrooms and dried mushrooms in water and cut them into thin strips. Fry the beaten egg yolk and egg white separately into sheets and cut them into thin strips. Halve the pine nuts.

3 Place the #1 patty on a damp cloth in a steamer and top it with the #2 prepared garnish and steam.

4 When the steamed patty cools, cut it into bite-sized pieces and serve with the vinegar-soy sauce.

16

Steamed Bean Curd

1 Mix the mashed bean curd and minced beef well with the seasoning.

2 Place the square patty in a steamer, top it with the garnish and steam.

Ingredients 5 eggs, 1 tbsp. salt, ¼ cup soy sauce, 1 tbsp. sugar, ⅔ cup water, 1 tsp. ginger juice, lettuce leaves

Method **1** Hard-boil the eggs in salted water for 12 minutes.

2 Rinse the boiled eggs in cold water and peel.

3 Simmer the peeled eggs with ⅔ cup water, ¼ cup soy sauce, 1 tbsp. sugar and ginger juice in a pot. When the liquid is almost evap-

orated, cook them on high heat until glazed.

4 Cool the eggs and cut them into bite-sized pieces. Serve on a platter with lettuce leaves and parsley.

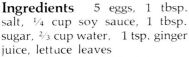

1 Hard-boil the eggs.

2 Rinse the eggs in cold water and peel.

Bean Curd in Soy Sauce
Tubut'wigimjorim (두부튀김조림)

Salted Bean Curd and Beef
Tubu Soegogijorim (두부 쇠고기조림)

Ingredients 2 cakes bean curd, 2 tbsp. salt, 5 tbsp. flour, 4 dried brown, oak mushrooms, 4 green peppers, 1 red pepper, 4 pieces fried bean curd, 4 cups broth, 1½ tbsp. sugar, 2 tbsp. rice wine, 2½ tbsp. soy sauce

Method 1 Pat the bean curd until dry with a cloth. Divide the bean curd into 8 equal parts and sprinkle them with salt.
2 Dip the bean curd pieces into flour and deep-fry them in oil on medium heat.
3 Scald the fried bean curd in boiling water, cover them with cold water and cut them into halves.
4 Scald the dried mushrooms slightly, remove the stems and cut them into halves.
5 Trim the stems to ⅓" in length on the green peppers and red pepper.
6 Boil the broth with the sugar, rice wine and soy sauce in a pot. Add the fried bean curd, deep-fried bean curd pieces and dried mushrooms and simmer. Then add the red pepper and green peppers and cook briefly so that the color does not change.

2 Cut the bean curd and dip the pieces into salt and flour.

4 Simmer the deep-fried pieces with the seasoning.

1 Sprinkle the bean curd with salt and gently press out the moisture.

Ingredients 1 cake bean curd, ¼ lb. beef, 2 oz. konyak: jellied potato-cake, 2 oz. carrot, 1 green bell pepper, 2 dried brown, oak mushrooms, 1 tbsp. frying oil, 2 tbsp. rice wine, 3 tbsp. soy sauce, 2 tbsp. sugar, ¾ cup water, ginger juice, black pepper.
Method 1 Cut the bean curd

3 Deep-fry the bean curd in oil on medium heat until golden brown.

into piece ¾"×2". Scald them in boiling salted water and rinse them in cold water.
2 Cut the beef, carrot and jellied potato-cake into pieces ¾"×2" and ¼" thick.
3 Halve the bell peppers and re-move the seeds. Cut them into the same size as the above ingredients.

5 Add the green peppers and cook slightly.

4 Soak the dried mushrooms in water and cut them into halves.
5 Fry the beef, carrot, dried mushroom and bean curd pieces in an oiled pan, add the water and bring to a boil. When the carrot is done, fry on high heat to finish the cooking. Correct the seasoning and add the bell pepper.

18

1 Scald the sliced bean curd in salt water.

2 Fry all the ingredients except the bell pepper adding water to boil.

3 When carrot gets cooked, finish the cooking on high heat. Then add the bell pepper, fry lightly and serve.

Ingredients 1 cup black beans, 4 tbsp. soy sauce, 3 tbsp. sugar, 4 cups water, 1 tsp. sesame seed, 1 tsp. sesame oil

Method **1** Wash the black beans and soak them in 4 cups water for 3 hours. Put the beans and the soaking water, 2 tbsp. soy sauce and 1½ tbsp. sugar in a pot and cook.

2 When the beans are tender, add the remaining soy sauce and sugar and simmer gently on medium heat.

3 When the beans are almost cooked, add the sesame oil and sesame seed and cook quickly on high heat until glazed.

Hint First simmer the beans with half of the seasoning and then add the remaining seasoning and cook quickly on high heat.

1 Boil the soaked black beans in water with the soy sauce and sugar.

2 Add the remaining seasoning and cook.

5-Color Egg Rolls
Talgyal Osaekmari (달걀 오색말이)

Ingredients   5 eggs, 2 oz. carrot, 2 oz. bean sprouts, 2 oz. spinach, 2 sheets laver, 2 oz. dried brown, oak mushrooms, salt, soy sauce, sesame oil, sugar

Method   1 Beat the whites of two eggs, fry them into a thin sheet, salt lightly and cut into thin strips.
2 Beat three eggs and the two egg yolks with a little salt.
3 Cut the carrot into thin strips, fry it with the sesame oil and season it with the salt.
4 Remove the hairlike roots from the bean sprouts and scald. Trim and scald the spinach. Squeeze out the water. Then mix each vegetable separately with the salt, sesame oil and sugar.
5 Soak the dried mushrooms in water and remove the stems. Cut them into thin strips and fry them with the soy sauce, sugar and sesame oil.
6 Pick any hard specks out of the laver. Place a sheet of laver on the bamboo mat. Then lay half of the carrot, bean sprouts, spinach, white strips and dried mushroom on the laver and roll it up as you would a jelly roll. Fill the other sheets of laver in the same fashion to make the rolls.
7 Fry the #2 beaten eggs on one side only into a thin sheet in an oiled square pan, place the laver roll on the egg and wrap in the egg sheet cooking it until well-done. Place the egg roll on a mat with a raised half-circle design and press it into a flowerlike shape.
8 Cut the #7 egg rolls into ¾″ lengths and serve them with the vinegar-soy sauce for dipping.

1 Fry the beaten egg whites into a sheet and cut it into thin strips.

2 Place the carrot, mushroom, egg white strips, bean sprouts and spinach on a sheet of laver and roll it up.

3 Place the laver roll on the egg sheet, roll it in a bamboo mat, press lightly to leave a design, and slice.

Egg and Spinach Rolls

Talgyal Shigŭmch'imari (달걀 시금치말이)

Ingredients   2 eggs, 1 tsp. cornstarch, ½ tbsp. water, ½ lb. spinach, 1 tsp. salt, ½ tsp. sugar, 1 tsp. sesame oil, MSG, 2 tbsp. soy sauce

Method   **1** Beat the eggs well.
2 Scald the spinach lightly in boiling salted water and rinse it in cold water. Squeeze out the water and season the spinach with the soy sauce, sugar and sesame oil.
3 Dissolve the cornstarch in ½tbsp. water and mix it with the beaten egg, MSG, sugar and salt.
4 Fry the beaten egg on one side only in a thick square pan. Place the scalded spinach on the egg sheet, roll it up and finish cooking. Make the other rolls in the same way.
5 Place the rolls on a kitchen board and cut them diagonally with a sharp knife. Serve with the soy sauce for dipping.

Hint   Do not put too much spinach on the egg sheet, and the rolls will look prettier when cut.

3 Place the seasoned spinach on the egg sheet.

1 Scald the spinach and mix it with the seasonings.

2 Fry the beaten egg in a fry pan.

4 Roll #3 and finish cooking.

Cold Cooked Bean Curd
Tubu Naengch'ae (두부 냉채)

Ingredients   1 cake bean curd, 1 tbsp. salt, 2 oz. ham, 2 oz. jellyfish, 1 cucumber, ½ carrot, 1 egg, ½ firm Korean pear, 3 tbsp. vinegar, 3 tbsp. chopped garlic, 1 tbsp. sugar, 1½ tsp. salt, ½ tsp. sesame oil, 3 tbsp. water, 1½ tsp. soy sauce

Method   1 Cut the bean curd into pieces 2″ thick and sprinkle with salt. Fry the pieces until golden brown and cut them into 2″ long strips.

2 Cut the ham into 2″ long strips.

3 Select a thin, green cucumber. Rub it with salt, clean and cut it into the same size as the ham. Remove the salt water from the jellyfish and scald it slightly in hot water (140°F). Cut it into 2″ long strips and marinate it in the vinegar and sugar.

4 Peel the pear and cut it into the same size as the ham. Soak it in sugar water to keep the color and drain.

5 Mix the bean curd and half of the cucumber and jellyfish strips.

6 Arrange the #5 mixture in the center of a plate and arrange the carrot, ham, cucumber, pear and egg strips around it. Serve with the garlic-vinegar sauce for dipping.

1 Sprinkle the bean curd pieces with salt and fry.

3 Make the garlic-vinegar sauce.

2 Cut all the ingredients into thick strips.

4 Arrange the ingredients attractively on a plate.

Rice
Gruel
Noodles

Bean Sprout Rice
K'ongnamulpap (콩나물밥)

Pine Mushroom Rice
Songibŏsŏtpap (송이버섯밥)

Ingredients   3 cups rice, ⅔ lb. bean sprouts, ¼ lb. beef, various seasonings, 3½ cup water, seasonging sauce

Method   1 Wash the rice and let it stand for 30 minutes before cooking. Trim and clean the bean sprouts.

2 Boil the bean sprouts in 3 cups salted water. Set aside the bean sprout water to use later for boiling the rice.

3 Cut the beef into thin strips, marinate in various seasonings and stir-fry in an oiled pan.

4 Mix the rice and fried beef and pour in the bean sprout liquid. Then boil the mixture.

5 When the rice boils, put the boiled bean sprouts on top and let them cook until well-steamed.

6 Stir the cooked rice, meat and sprouts lightly and serve in a bowl. By seasoning this mixture well a delicious mixed-rice dish results.

1 Boil the bean sprouts in salted water.

2 Fry the seasoned beef.

3 Bring the rice and fried beef to a boil and then add the bean sprouts.

Ingredients   A. 10 pine mushrooms

B. 3 cups rice, 3 cups water, 3 tbsp. rice wine, 1 tbsp. soy sauce, ¼ tsp. salt

C. ½ lb. chicken, 2 tsp. soy sauce, 2 tsp. rice wine

Method   1 Wash the rice.

2 Peel the pine mushrooms and cut them into four equal parts.

3 Cut the chicken into bite-sized pieces and season with the **C** ingredients.

4 Place the prepared rice, pine mushrooms and seasoned chicken in a pot and stir to mix evenly. Pour the remaining **B** ingredients into the pot and boil the mixture

on high heat for 10 minutes. Then reduce the heat and cook 10 minutes more until the rice is well done.

Hint   If you wash the pine mushrooms, they change color. Instead, peel, slice and then cook them.

Pine Mushroom Rice

Bean Sprout Rice

1 Peel the pine mushrooms.

2 Cut the pine mushrooms into four equal parts.

3 Season the chicken with the soy sauce and rice wine.

4 Put the rice in a pot and then add the soy sauce and salt.

5 Add #2 and #3 to #4 and cook.

1 Wash the glutinous rice, rice and sorghum.

Ingredients　2 cups glutinous rice, 2 cups regular rice, 1 cup glutinous sorghum, 1 cup glutinous millet, ½ cup dried black beans,. ½ cup dried sweet beans, salt

Method　1 Wash the regular rice and glutinous rice and drain.

2 Clean the sorghum rubbing it well in one's hands until the rinse water is no longer red.

3 Soak the black beans in water and drain. Rinse the sweet beans, boil and drain setting aside the cooking water for later use.

2 Wash the black beans and boil the sweet beans.

3 Boil all the ingredients, add the millet evenly and cook until well-done.

4 Wash the millet and drain.

5 Mix all the ingredients except the millet. Place the mixture in a pot and cover it with the rice water and sweet bean water, add a little salt and boil.

6 When the rice comes to a boil, add the millet evenly, reduce the fire and cook for 10 minutes more until the rice is well-done.

Hint　Mix the grains and water at the ratio of 1 to 1. Salt may be added up to 1 percent of the rice water.

25

Vegetables to Mix with Rice
Pibimpap (비빔밥)

Ingredients **A.** 2 cups rice, 2 cups water **B.** 2 oz. beef, 1 tbsp. soy sauce, ½ tsp. sesame oil, ½ tsp. sesame salt, green onion, garlic, black pepper **C.** ½ lb. bean sprouts, 1 tsp. salt, 1 tsp. sesame oil, green onion, garlic **D.** ¼ lb. boiled bracken, 1 tsp. soy sauce, ½ tsp. sesame oil, ½ tsp. sesame salt, green onion, garlic **E.** 1 cucumber, 1 tsp. salt, sesame oil **F.** ½ cake mung bean gelatin, salt, sesame oil **G.** ¼ lb. scalded bellflower roots, 1 tsp. soy sauce, ½ tsp. sesame oil, 1 tsp. sesame salt, 1 tsp. salt **H.** 2 eggs **I.** 2 lettuce leaves, seasoning sauce, 1 tsp. sesame oil

Method **1** Shred and scald the bellflower roots. Fry them seasoning with the **G** ingredients.
2 Cut the beef into thin strips. Fry it seasoning with the **B** ingredients. Cut the bracken into 2" lengths. Fry it seasoning with the **C** ingredients.
3 Cut the cucumber into half-moon-shaped pieces and sprinkle it with salt. Squeeze out the moisture, season it with the **E** ingredients and fry lightly.
4 Scald the bean sprouts in ½ cup boiling salted water, drain and mix them with the **C** ingredients. Cut the mung bean gelatin into thin strips and mix it with the **F** ingredients.
5 Wash and cook the rice.
6 Fry the egg until it is soft-set.
7 Serve the prepared vegetables with seasoned red pepper paste, the rice and soup.

1 Scald the bellflower roots and fry them with the sesame oil and salt to taste.

2 Cut the beef into thin strips and fry it with the seasoning.

3 Cut the scalded bracken and fry it with the seasoning.

4 Sprinkle the cucumber with salt, squeeze out the moisture and fry lightly.

5 Mix the scalded bean sprouts with the sesame oil. Cut the mung bean gelatin into thick strips.

1 Grind the soaked rice; then add the black sesame seeds and grind again in a blender.

Ingredients 1 cup black sesame seeds, 2 cups rice, 10 cups water, salt, sugar, powdered pine nuts

Method **1** Clean and soak the black sesame seeds in water. Crush the seeds with a mortar and pestle to remove any hulls. Rinse and stir-fry to dry.
2 Soak and grind the rice with 3 cups water. Add the black sesame

Pine Nut Gruel
Chatchuk (잣죽)

Black Sesame Seed Gruel
Hugimjajuk (흑임자죽)

1 Cut the jujubes into thin strips and marinate them in syrup.

2 Grind the rice in a blender.

3 Boil #1 and #2 stirring well.

Ingredients 2 cups rice, 1 cup pine nuts, 10 cups water, 5 jujubes, salt, sugar syrup

Method **1** Soak the rice in water and let it stand.

2 Remove the tops from the pine nuts and grind them with 1 cup water in a blender.

3 Pit the jujubes and cut them into thin strips. Marinate them in honey or syrup.

4 Grind the soaked rice with 2 cups water in a blender.

5 Boil the ground rice with the remaining water in a pot. When it gets somewhat thick, add the pine nut liquid slowly stirring as you pour to mix it well and bring the mixture to a boil.

2 Boil the #1 mixture in a pot stirring it well with a wooden spoon.

seeds and grind the mixture again.

3 Boil the #2 mixture with the remaining water on low heat in a thick pan stirring often with a wooden spoon.

Hint Season the gruel with sugar and salt at the table.

Black Sesame Seed Gruel

Abalone Porridge
Chŏnbokchuk (전복죽)

Rice-Cake Soup
Ttŏkkuk (떡국)

Ingredients 3 abalones, 1 cup rice, 1 tbsp. sesame oil, 6 cups water, 1 tbsp. salt

Method **1** Clean the abalones well with a brush, remove the shells and entrails, and cut the abalone meat into thin strips.

2 Grind the soaked rice well in a mortar, add 4 cups water and strain. Save the strained water for later use.

3 Fry the abalone meat with the sesame oil in a heavy pan. Then add the **#2** rice and cook thoroughly.

4 Add the remaining water to **#3** and simmer on low heat until the rice becomes thick. Add the rice-straining water and bring to a boil again.

5 When the porridge comes to a boil, season it with soy sauce and salt to taste.

Hint **1** If you add the rice-straining water from the start, the porridge will scorch too easily.

2 You must simmer the porridge a long time on low heat because the porridge bubbles over if boiled too quickly on high heat.

1 Cut the abalone meat and grind the rice in a mortar.

2 Add the water to the ground rice and strain.

3 Boil the fried abalones and rice with the water.

4 Add the **#2** rice-straining water and simmer.

Ingredients 5 sticks of rice cake, ¼lb. beef, 2 oz. ground beef, 1 egg, 1 tbsp. laver powder, 1 green onion, 1 tbsp. soy sauce, 1 tbsp. chopped green onion, 1 tsp. sesame salt, 1 tsp. chopped garlic, 1 tsp. sesame oil, flour

Method **1** Leave the soft sticks of rice cake out overnight to harden; cut them diagonally into oval pieces when hard.

2 Cut the beef into thin strips and season.

3 Season and shape the ground beef into meatballs ¾″ in diameter. Dip them into flour, then into beaten egg and fry.

4 Fry the beaten egg into a thin sheet and cut it into thin strips.

5 Fry the **#2** beef in a pot and boil it with 8 cups water.

6 When the meat flavor per-

1 Cut the beef into thin strips and fry in an oiled pot.

2 Add the water to **#1** and bring to a boil.

3 When the **#2** soup boils, add the rice cake pieces and boil.

Rice-Cake Soup

meates the broth, add the rice-cake slices and bring to a boil.

7 Season the soup with the soy sauce and salt and add the diagonally cut green onion. Place the rice-cake soup in a bowl and top it with the egg strips, meatballs and powdered laver.

Hint Instead of the egg strips you may add beaten egg to the soup when it is boiling hot.

Ingredients **A.** ¼ lb. beef, ½ cake bean curd, 3 tbsp. beaten egg, ¼ lb. mung bean sprouts, ⅓ zucchini, 2 dried brown, oak mushrooms **B.** 2 tbsp. pine nuts **C.** 6 cups meat stock, 1 tbsp. soy sauce, 1 tsp. salt, MSG **D.** ½ tbsp. soy sauce, ½ tsp. salt, 1 green onion, 3 cloves garlic, 1 tsp. sesame salt, sesame oil, black pepper **E.** 1½ cup flour, 1 tsp. salt, ½ cup warm water **F.** 3 tbsp. soy sauce, 1 tsp. sugar, 2 tsp. vinegar, green onion, garlic, sesame salt

Method 1 Mince the beef finely and fry it in a fry pan.
2 Squeeze the water from the bean curd. Scald and drain the mung bean sprouts, chop them finely and squeeze out the water.
3 Remove the stems from the dried mushrooms and chop them. Cut the zucchini into thin strips and sprinkle it with salt; squeeze out the water and fry lightly.
4 Add the **D** seasonings to **#1**, **#2** and **#3** ingredients and mix well.
5 Knead the flour water and salt to make a thick dough. Put the dough into a vinyl bag and let it stand for 30 minutes.
6 Roll the dough into thin sheets and cut them into 2" square pieces. Place the **#4** mixture and a pine nut on each square, pinch the four edges together tightly to make the square-shaped "ravioli".
7 Boil the **C** ingredients and add the **#6** dumplings. When the soup comes to a boil, add ½ cup cold broth and bring it to a boil again.
8 Top the soup with the egg strips and green onion and serve with the seasoned vinegar sauce.

1 Mix the fried beef and all the ingredients with the seasoning.

2 Place the #1 mixture and a pine nut on each square and pinch the four edges together tightly.

Thin Noodles on a Wicker Tray
Ch'aebansomyŏn (채반소면)

Noodles with Beans
K'ongguksu (콩국수)

Ingredients ⅓ lb. thin noodles, 1 egg, ¼ lb. jellied crab meat, ½ cucumber, 3 stone mushrooms, 2 small green onions, 5 chrysanthemum leaves, 2 tbsp. soy sauce, 1 tbsp. rice wine, 1 tbsp. sugar, black pepper, 3 cups anchovy-kelp broth

Method   1 Boil the thin noodles briefly and rinse them in cold water.

1 Roll the noodles around the tips of chopsticks and place them on chrysanthemum leaves on a wicker tray.

Ingredients   1 cup dried soybeans, 4 or 5 cups water, ¼ lb. noodles, 1 cucumber, salt, ½ tomato, 1 egg

Method   1 Wash the soybeans and let them stand overnight. Boil for 15 minutes and rinse them in cold water to remove the hulls. Grind the soybeans with four or five cups water in a blender and

Roll the boiled noodles around the tips of chopsticks and place them on chrysanthemum leaves on a wicker tray.

2 Fry the egg yolk and white separately into sheet and cut them into thin strips. Cut the cucumber into thin strips and shred the jellied crab meat finely.

3 Boil three anchovies and one

2 Cut all the ingredients into thin strips and shred the jellied crab meat.

season them with salt. (Adding sesame seeds to the soybeans in the blender gives nice flavor.)

2 Cut the cucumber and egg sheet into thin strips. Divide the tomato into eight sections.

3 Cook the noodles in boiling water, rinse them in cold water and drain. Place the noodles in a wide dish, pour the soybean puree over them and top it with the cucumber, egg strips and tomato.

piece of kelp with three cups water. Pour the boiled liquid into a bowl and let it cool to make the broth.

4 Add the seasoning to the **#3** broth to make the seasoning sauce.

5 Top the rolls of noodles with the sliced stone mushrooms and arrange them with the **#2** ingredients on a wicker tray. Serve with the seasoning sauce.

3 Add the seasoning to the kelp broth to make the seasoning sauce.

Serve with salt.

1 Boil the soaked soybeans for 15 minutes.

2 Grind the **#1** soybeans with water in a blender.

3 Strain the ground soybeans and season them with salt.

Noodles with Beans

Thin Noodles on a Wicker Tray

Rice Cakes
Sweets
Beverages

Half-Moon-Shaped Rice Cake
Songp'yŏn (송편)

Sweet Rice
Yakshik (약식)

1 Divide the rice flour into three equal parts. Knead each part into soft dough.

2 Fill the dough pieces with the chestnut, and jujube stuffings and make the half-moon-shaped rice cakes.

Ingredients   5 cups rice, 1 tbsp. salt, food colors, 2 oz. mugwort, 10 chestnuts, ½ cup sesame seeds, 10 jujubes, 1 cup sweet bean flour, 1 tsp. salt, 2 tbsp. honey, 2 tbsp. sesame oil, ½ cup sugar

Method   **1** Wash the rice, soak it for a while and drain. Grind the soaked rice very finely adding salt and strain.
2 Peel the chestnuts, boil them and put through a sieve. Pit and chop the jujubes finely. Fry the sesame seeds and simmer the sweet bean flour with ½ cup sugar. Then mix each ingredient with salt and honey.
3 Divide the ground rice into three equal parts. Add the food color to one-third along with boiling water and knead it into dough. Add boiled chopped mugwort to the second part and knead. Add boiling water to the rest as it is and knead it into dough.
4 Fill the dough pieces with the #**2** filling and shape them into half-moon-shaped rice cakes.
5 Steam the half-moon rice cakes and brush them with the sesame oil.

Sweet Rice

Ingredients   5 cups glutinous rice, 2 cups (dark brown) sugar, 3 tbsp. sesame oil, 3 tbsp. soy sauce, 10 chestnuts, 20 jujubes, 2 tbsp. raisin, ¼ cup pine nuts.

Method   **1** Soak the glutinous rice thoroughly in water and drain. Steam it with the chestnuts in a steamer. When steaming hot, sprinkle with salt and then dash cold water over the steamed rice and steam once more.
2 Pit the jujubes and cut them into 4 pieces.
3 Remove the tops of the pine nuts.
4 Scoop steamed rice out of the steamer while still hot and mix it with the jujubes, raisins, pine nuts, dark brown sugar, soy sauce and sesame oil evenly. Steam the mixture in greased pans in an electric oven at 450°F for 20 mi-

32

Glutinous Rice Cake
Injŏlmi (인절미)

1 Pound the steamed glutinous rice in a mortar.

2 Dip the pounded rice cake into water to shape into pieces and cut.

Ingredients   5 cups glutinous rice, 1 tbsp. salt, ½ cup dried sweet beans, ½ cup dried yellow bean flour, ½ cup dried green bean flour

Method   1 Soak the glutinous rice in water thoroughly and drain. Place it on a damp cloth in a steamer, leaving the center empty, and steam well. Sprinkle with salt water while steaming and stir with a wooden scoop.

2 Place the steamed glutinous rice in a mortar while still hot and pound until smooth.

3 Soak the sweet beans in water and remove the skins completely. Steam the beans and mash when hot. Push the mashed sweet beans through a thick sieve making a

sweet bean puree. Wash the dried beans and drain, fry and grind them finely into the bean flour.

4 Remove the pounded rice cake from the mortar by dipping your hands in water; place it on a flat board. Shape it into thin, flat rectangles. Cut the rectangles into 1⅔" long pieces and dip the rice cake pieces into the bean flour.

---

nutes if an oven is available.

5 Otherwise, place the mixed rice in a bowl and put the bowl into a steamer containing boiling water and steam. Fluff up the mixed rice several times while steaming.

6 When the rice gets tender, add the pine nuts, jujubes and raisins and pack the rice into greased jello-molds or custard cups. Then turn the packed molds upside down to remove the sweet rice and serve.

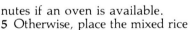

1 Soak the glutinous rice in water and steam it with the chestnuts in a steamer.

3 Stir the mixed rice up and down when steaming-hot sprinkling with salted water.

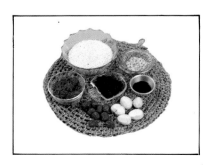

2 Pit the jujubes and remove the tops of the pine nuts.

4 When the rice is done, add all the ingredients and mix well.

5-Color Rice Cake Balls
Osaekkyŏngdan (오색경단)

3-Color Sweet Dumplings
Samsaekchuak (삼색주악)

Ingredients 5 cups glutinous rice, 2 cups dried sweet beans, 1 cup sugar, 1 tsp. salt, 10 chestnuts, 20 jujubes, ½ cup black sesame seeds, ½ cup soy bean flour, ½ cup cinnamon powder

Method 1 Wash the glutinous rice and soak it in water. Crush it finely adding salt and sift.

2 After cleaning soak the sweet beans in water and let them stand overnight. Boil, mash and sieve them. Squeeze the liquid from the sweet bean puree and simmer it with sugar to make the filling.

3 Peel the chestnuts, cut them into fine strips and soak them in cold water. Pit the jujubes and cut them into thin strips.

4 Remove the skins by rubbing the black sesame seeds together in water. Stir-fry and crush them.

5 Wash and dry the beans. Fry until golden brown, crush finely and sift them.

6 Knead the glutinous rice flour mixed with boiling water and fill small pieces of the dough with the simmered sweet beans to make small balls. Boil the balls in boiling water, rinse them in cold water, drain and let them cool. Then roll each ball in the chestnut strips, jujube strips, cinnamon, black sesame seeds or soy flour.

1 Knead the glutinous rice flour into dough.

2 Simmer the sweet bean puree with sugar.

3 Fill the dough with the sweet bean mixture to make the balls.

4 Boil the balls in boiling water and rinse them in cold water.

5 Roll the #4 balls in soy flour.

Ingredients 5 cups glutinous rice, 1 tbsp. salt, 20 jujubes, 1 tsp. cinnamon, 1 tsp. honey, food coloring (pink, green), 3 cups frying oil, ½ cup honey or syrup

Method 1 Wash the glutinous rice and soak it in water. Drain, grind finely and sift. Divide the sifted rice into three equal parts.

2 Dissolve each food coloring separately in water.

3 Leave one-third of the rice flour white, add the food coloring separately to the other two parts of

Sesame Cakes
Kkaegangjŏng (깨강정)

Ingredients ⅓ lb. rootlets of ginseng, 1 carrot, ½ Korean white radish, 2 tbsp. salt, 1 cup sugar, 1 cup water, 1 cup light syrup

Method **1** Wash the ginseng rootlets well.

2 Cut the carrot and radish into pieces ¼" thick by ⅓" × 2⅓". Scald in boiling salted water and rinse them in cold water.

3 Simmer the ginseng rootlets and the **#2** ingredients in the sugar water on low heat in a thick pan. Then add the light syrup and cook slowly until no syrup remains and the rootlets are sticky.

Ingredients ½ cup white sesame seeds, ½ cup black sesame seeds, ½ cup light-brown syrup, ⅓ cup sugar

Method **1** Clean the white and black sesame seeds separately. Stir-fry them until plump.

2 Mix the syrup and sugar in a bowl and cook until clear. Mix the white sesame and black sesame each separately with the boiled syrup and roll out the mixture into thin sheets.

3 Place the black sesame sheet on the white sesame sheet and roll them together before they cool.

4 Roll in mat and slice into small circles.

1 Mix the white sesame and black sesame each separately with the boiled syrup.

3 Place the black sesame sheet on the white sesame sheet and roll them together tightly in the bamboo mat.

2 Roll out each mixture into a thin sheet.

4 Cut the roll into bite-sized circles.

1 Mix all the ingredients with grain syrup and knead into a soft dough.

2 Shape the dough into small patterned cakes using the patterned-cake mold.

Nine-Section Dish
Kujŏlp'an (구절판)

Ingredients   **A.** 3 oz. beef, 2 tsp. soy sauce, 1 tsp. chopped green onion, ½ tsp. chopped garlic, 1 tsp. sesame oil, ½ tsp. sesame salt, 1 tsp. sugar
B. ⅓ lb. shrimp, salt, sugar, vinegar
C. ½ cucumber, 3 oz. carrot, 2 tsp. salt, 2 tsp. sesame oil
D. 3 oz. bamboo shoots, 1 tsp. salt, 1 tsp. sesame oil
E. 6 dried brown, oak mushrooms, 1 tsp. soy sauce, ½ tsp. sugar, sesame oil
F. 1 egg, salt
G. 3 oz. bellflower roots, 1 tsp. salt, ½ tsp. sesame oil, ½ tsp. garlic
H. 1 cup flour, 1 cup water, salt
I. 1 tbsp. chopped pine nuts

Method   **1** Remove the entrails from the shrimp. Insert toothpicks into the bodies of the shrimp and scald them in boiling water; remove the shells. Cut the flesh into thin strips and mix with the salt, sugar and vinegar.
2 Cut the beef into thin strips, season it with the **A** ingredients and fry.
3 Soak the dried mushrooms in water and cut them into thin strips. Season them with the **E** ingredients and fry.
4 Cut the carrot and cucumber into thin strips and sprinkle them with salt. Squeeze out the water and fry. Cut the bamboo shoots into thin strips and fry.
5 Fry the beaten egg into a thin sheet and cut it into 2" long strips.
6 Scald and shred the bellflower roots finely. Fry in the sesame oil and mix them with the **G** ingredients.
7 Mix and beat the **H** ingredients until the batter is smooth. Drop the batter by spoonfuls onto a hot lightly oiled fry pan to make the thin pancakes.
8 Layer the pancakes in the center section of the 9-section dish topping each one with a little powdered pine nut. Then arrange the eight other prepared ingredients in the other sections.

1 Remove the shells from the boiled shrimps and season.

2 Cut the beef into thin strips, season and fry them.

Sweet Rice Drink
Shik'ye (식혜)

Ingredients 3 cups glutinous rice, 3 cups malt powder, 3 tbsp. pine nuts, 3 cups sugar, 40 cups water

Method 1 Pour 40 cups of water over the powdered malt and let it stand for one night. Stir and press the malt-powder so that the malt-flavor seeps into the liquid. Strain the malt-water through a fine sieve and allow the malt-water to settle leaving a clear liquid.

2 Soak the glutinous rice in water and drain. Steam it in a steamer sprinkling some more water over the top when steaming-hot to produce more steam and sticky rice.

3 Place the steamed rice in a large bowl to cool. Add the clear malt-water to the bowl and stir it well. Then leave it at 100° F, until it ferments. (Or let it stand for two and a half hours or three hours in thermal rice container.)

4 When four or five grains of rice float to the top, take the liquid out of the container. As it cools, all grains of rice will float to the top. At this time, separate the grains from the liquid.

5 Wash the grains of rice in water and drain.

6 Simmer the fermented rice liquid and add the sugar to taste. Let it cool and store it in glass bottles.

7 Place the sweet rice drink in individual serving bowls and top it with some grains of the fermented rice.

Hint Add a little ginger juice and float some minced citron with the grains of rice on the liquid for an even more delicious drink.

2 Add the clear malt-water to the steamed glutinous rice and stir well.

1 Press the malt hard in the water and strain the malt-water through a fine sieve.

3 When grains of rice float to the top, separate the rice and the liquid. Wash the grains of rice and simmer the liquid.

3 Cut the remaining ingredients into thin strips.

4 Mix the pancake batter.

5 Fry the batter.

Persimmon Punch
Sujŏnggwa (수정과)

Honey-Coated Pear
Paesuk (배숙)

Ingredients   10 dried persimmons, ⅓ lb. ginger, ¼ oz. stick cinnamon, 13 cups water, 2 cups sugar, 2 tbsp. pine nuts

Method   **1** Remove the seeds from the dried persimmons and replace them with four or five pine nuts.
2 Wash and scrape the ginger and slice it thinly. Simmer the ginger and stick cinnamon with the water until the strong taste draws well. Add the sugar and briefly boil again.
3 Pour this liquid through a fine sieve.
4 Pour this syrup over the dried persimmons in a large bowl.
5 When the persimmons are soft, serve them adding the syrupy liquid and sprinkling whole pine nuts on the top of each serving.

1 Remove the seeds from the dried persimmons and replace them with the pine nuts.

2 Simmer the ginger and cinnamon until the strong taste draws well.

Honey-Coated Pear

3 Cover the persimmons with the spicy syrup and store the remaining syrup separately.

Ingredients   2 firm Korean pears, ¼ oz. stick cinnamon, ¼ lb. ginger, 10 cups water, 1½ cup sugar, 3 tbsp. black pepper seeds, pine nuts
Method   **1** Scrape the ginger and slice thinly. Boil the ginger and cinnamon with the water.

Rice-Cake Fruit Cup
Ttŏk'wach'ae (떡화채)

1 Boil the sliced ginger and stick cinnamon with the water.

2 Divide the pear into eight equal sections, remove the center core and press in the black pepper seeds.

3 Place the pear pieces in a pot, sprinkle with sugar and allow them to stand for a while.

4 Pour the **#1** syrup over the pears and simmer on low heat.

2 Peel the pear and divide it into eight equal sections. Remove the center core and press three or five black pepper seeds into the pear pieces. Sprinkle with sugar and allow them to stand for a while. Add the **#1** syrup and simmer until the pear looks glazed. To serve, sprinkle whole pine nuts on top.

Ingredients   ½ cup glutinous rice flour, ½ cup rice flour, ½ tsp. salt, 2½ cup water, ½ cup sugar, 1 knob ginger, raisins, pine nuts, 1 apple, 1 plum, 1peach

Method   **1** Knead the rice flour, salt and hot water into a soft dough. Shape the dough into ginko nut-sized pieces. Place some raisins and pine nuts on each piece

1 Knead the rice flour, salt and hot water into a dough.

and re-shape into round balls.
2 Boil the balls in boiling water and rinse them in cold water.
3 Boil the water with the sugar and ginger to make a syrup and let it cool. Then remove the ginger from the syrup. Slice the fruits into bite-sized pieces. Place the rice cake balls, fruit pieces in a bowl and pour on the syrup to serve.

2 Slice the fruits into bite-sized pieces.

3 Boil the water with the sugar and ginger and let it cool.

43

Watermelon Punch
Subak'wach'ae (수박화채)

Ingredients 1 watermelon, 1 bottle cider, ½ cup brandy, 1 tbsp. pine nuts, 1 cup sugar, 1 cup water

Method 1 Cut the upper part of the watermelon in a sawtooth-design. Scoop out watermelon balls with a melon baller.
2 Boil 1 cup water with 1 cup sugar to make the syrup.
3 Soak the watermelon balls in the syrup. Wrap the remaining watermelon in a cloth and squeeze out the juice.
4 Place the watermelon balls, syrup, cider, brandy and #3 watermelon juice in the watermelon shell and float ice pieces on top.
5 Serve the watermelon punch sprinkled with pine nuts in a bowl.

1 Cut the watermelon in a sawtooth-design.

3 Wrap the remaining watermelon in a cloth and squeeze out the juice.

2 Soak the watermelon balls in the syrup.

4 Mix #2, #3, brandy, cider and the syrup.

1 Layer the grapes and sugar in a large jar.

44

Grape Wine
P'odoju (포도주)

Plum Wine
Chaduju (자두주)

Ingredients   1⅓ lb. grape, ¼ lb. sugar, 1½ liter Korean soju (a strong rice-wine)

Method   1 Wash the grapes. Pat dry with a cloth. Layer the grapes and sugar in a large glass jar and let them stand for a day.

Add a little Korean wine to dissolve the sugar and seal.

2 Two months later, take the grapes out of the jar and let them drip through a fine sieve. Place the strained grape wine in the bottle and seal.

1 Layer the plums and sugar, let them stand overnight and add Korean soju.

Plum Wine

Ingredients   1⅓ lb. plum, ¼ lb. sugar, 1½ liter Korean soju (a strong rice-wine)

Method   1 Wash the plums and pat dry with a cloth. Layer the plums and sugar in a large jar.

2 Allow the plums to stand overnight and then add Korean wine to the #1 mixture.

3 When the plums ferment completely (one month later), place the plums over a fine sieve and let them drip. Place the strained plum wine in a bottle and seal.

2 Two months later, let the grape liquid drip through a fine sieve.

Apple Wine
Sagwaju (사과주)

Ingredients 4 apples, ¼ lb. sugar, 1½ liter Korean soju

Method 1 Wash the apples well and dry them. Cut each apple into eight equal sections.

2 Layer the apples and sugar in a large jar and let them stand for two days. Then add 3 times as much Korean wine as the marinated apple pieces.

3 When the apples ferment (three months later), place the apple pieces over a fine sieve letting all the juice drip out. Place the strained apple wine in the bottle and seal.

Hint It is good to use a high proof alcohol, but Korean soju (a strong rice wine) is generally used.

3 Add 3 times as much Korean wine as the #2 mixture.

1 Wash the apples and dry them. Divide each apple into eight sections.

2 Layer the apples and sugar in a large jar.

4 Place the fermented apples over a fine sieve (three months later) and let the juice drip out.

Kimchi
Basic Side Dishes
Basic Sauces

Whole Cabbage Kimchi
T'ongbaech'ugimch'i (통배추김치)

Ingredients 2 heads Chinese cabbages, 2 cups coarse salt, 1 Korean white radish, 1 cup red pepper powder, ⅓ cup tiny salted shrimp, 2 knobs ginger, 1 head garlic, 1 large green onion, ¼ bundle very thin green onion, ⅓ lb. fresh oyster, ⅓ bundle watercress, 4 tbsp. salt, ¼ bundle Indian mustard leaf, red pepper threads

Method 1 Trim the roots from the cabbages. Cut each cabbage lengthwise into two sections.
2 Make a brine with 10 cups water and 1 cup salt and soak the cabbage sections in the brine. Drain, sprinkle with the salt and let stand.
3 When the cabbages are well-salted and a bit limp, rinse thoroughly in cold water and drain.
4 Cut one-third of the radish into thin strips. Cut both kinds of green onions, the watercress stems and Indian mustard leaf into ¾" lengths.
5 Remove the shells from the fresh oysters and clean with salt water. Chop the salted shrimp, garlic and ginger.
6 Mix the red pepper powder well with the salted shrimp juice. Add the mixture to the radish strips and mix well until the reddish color is set. Then add the chopped shrimp, garlic, green onion, ginger, oysters, small green onion, Indian mustard leaf and watercress and mix well. Season with salt.
7 Pack the #6 seasoned mixture between each leaf of the wilted cabbage. Cut the remaining radish into large pieces and mix it with the seasoned mixture.
8 Place the stuffed cabbages and radish pieces in a large crock and cover the top with cabbage leaves. Weigh it down with a clean, heavy stone.

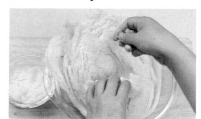

1 Soak the cabbages in salt water and drain. Sprinkle with salt and let stand.

2 Cut the radish, green onions and watercress and season.

3 Pack the seasoned mixture between each leaf of the cabbage.

48

Wrapped-Up Kimchi
Possamgimch'i (보쌈김치)

1 Soak the cabbage in salt water.

2 Cut all the ingredients and season.

3 Pack the **#2** stuffing between each leaf.

Ingredients   1 head Chinese cabbage, 1 piece Korean white radish, 1 piece carrot, ½ bundle watercress, ½ octopus, 3 chestnuts, 2 dried brown, oak mushrooms, 2 stone mushrooms, ¼ pear, 1 cup coarse salt, 1 green onion, 2 cloves garlic, 1 knob ginger, 1 tbsp. pine nuts, red pepper threads, ½ cup red pepper powder, 2 tbsp. salted soused shrimp, 2 tbsp. salted anchovies, 1 tbsp. sugar, 2 oz. oyster

Method   1 Remove the outer leaves from the cabbage and halve it lengthwise. Soak it in salt water and let it stand for 6 hours.
2 Cut the radish, carrot and pear

into 1″ × 1¼″ square by ¼″ thick slices.
3 Soak the stone mushrooms and dried mushrooms in water and clean. Cut them into thin strips.
4 Remove the roots and the leaves from the watercress and cut the stems into 1¼″ pieces. Slice the chestnuts into flat pieces.
5 Clean the octopus rubbing it with salt and cut it into 1¼″ lengths. Cut the green onion, garlic and ginger into thin strips.
6 Wash the salted cabbage and drain. Cut the stem area into 2⅓″ pieces. Place the stem pieces on the outer leaves and wrap them

temporarily in the leaves.
7 Mix **#2, #3, #4, #5** and oysters with the red pepper powder so that the ingredients pick up the reddish color. Season with the salted shrimp juice and salt, add the red pepper threads and pine nuts and mix well.
8 Pack the **#7** stuffing between each **#6** stem piece and this time wrap them firmly in the outer cabbage leaves.
9 Put the wrapped cabbage bundles one by one in a crock, pour the salt water over them and weigh them down with a heavy stone.

49

White Cabbage Kimchi
Paekkimch'i (백김치)

1 Sprinkle the cabbage with salt and let it stand.

2 Mix the sliced ingredients with the seasoning.

3 Pack the seasoned stuffing between the leaves of cabbage.

Ingredients   2 heads Chinese cabbages, 1 bundle watercress, 1 Korean white radish, 4 small green onions, 5 stone mushrooms, 1 pear, 5 jujubes, 3 chestnuts, ½ cup oysters, ⅓ octopus, 2 tbsp. salt, 1 head garlic, 3 knobs ginger, red pepper thread, 5 tbsp. salted soused shrimp, 2 tbsp. salted anchovies, 1 tbsp. pine nuts, MSG, 2 cups coarse salt,

Method   **1** Halve the cabbages lengthwise. Soak them in salt water for 6 hours and rinse them in cold water. Drain.
2 Cut the watercress and small green onion into 1⅔" lengths. Cut the trimmed stone mushrooms, chestnuts and jujubes into thin strips.
3 Cut the pear, garlic, ginger and half of radish into thin strips. Cut the rest of the radish into large pieces and sprinkle it with salt.
4 Wash the octopus rubbing it with salt and cut it into ¼" thick pieces. Wash well and rinse.
5 Remove the shells from the oysters, wash well and dry them off. Combine 1 cup of water and salted soused shrimp to make the salt brine.

6 Cut the red pepper thread enough so that they do not get tangled.
7 Mix the vegetable strips, octopus, oysters, pine nuts and red pepper thread thoroughly with the salt and MSG.
8 Pack the seasoned stuffing between each leaf of cabbage and wrap the cabbage with the outer leaves. Layer the cabbage bundles and radish pieces in a large crock and pour the #5 salt brine over them.

Radish Kimchi

50

Radish Kimchi
Yolmugimch'i (열무김치)

Water-Kimchi with Fresh Ginseng
Susamnabakkimch'i (수삼나박김치)

Ingredients   3 bundles young Korean white radish leaves, 1 bundle small green onion , 2 heads garlic, 1 knob ginger, 2 Korean green peppers, 2 red peppers, ½ round onion, powdered glutinous rice, 1 cup coarse salt

Method   **1** Trim the young radish leaves and cut them into 2¾″ lengths. Soak them in salt water, wash and drain.

2 Wash the green onion, garlic and ginger. Cut the green onion into 2″ lengths. Chop the garlic and ginger. Cut the round onion into thin strips.

3 Remove the stems and the seeds from the green peppers and red peppers and cut them diagonally.

4 Add the #2 and #3 ingredients to the salted radish leaves and mix well. Boil the glutinous rice with water into a thin paste-like gruel. Season the gruel with salt and let it cool.

5 Place the #4 radish kimchi in a crock and pour the #4 paste-gruel over it. To serve, put a mixture of kimchi and liquid into a dish.

Hint   A flour gruel can be used instead of the glutinous rice gruel.

1 Trim the young radish leaves and cut them into 2¾″ lengths.

2 Add the green peppers, red peppers, ginger and garlic and mix well.

1 Peel and trim the fresh ginseng.

2 Slice the ginseng, radish, carrot and cucumber.

Ingredients   4 roots fresh ginseng, ⅓ Korean white radish, 1 firm Korean pear, ½ carrot, 1 cucumber, 3 tbsp. coarse salt, 3 tbsp. sugar, ½ cup water, vinegar

Method   **1** Peel the fresh ginseng. Remove the fine roots. Clean well and dry them off.

2 Cut the radish, carrot and cucumber into the same size as the ginseng pieces.

3 Add vinegar and sugar to the water and stir until the sugar dis-

3 Mix the #2 ingredients with the vinegar, sugar and water.

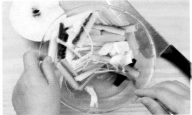
4 Add the sliced pear to the #3 mixture.

solves. Pour the liquid into a bowl and add the undried ginseng, radish, cucumber and carrot pieces.

4 Peel the pear, cut it the same size as the ginseng and add it to the #3 mixture.

Hint   When kimchi ripens into a sweet, vinegarish and salty dish, one can enjoy the true, refreshing kimchi flavor.

51

Whole Radish Kimchi
Alt'arigimch'i (알타리김치)

Radish Water-Kimchi
Tongch'imi (동치미)

Radish Water-Kimchi

Ingredients 2 bundles of small Korean white radishes, 2 oz. small green onion, 1 cup coarse salt, 1 cup red pepper powder, 3 green onions, 1 head garlic, 3 knobs ginger, 5 tbsp. salted soused anchovies, 1 tbsp. sugar

Method **1** Trim the whole radishes and remove the outer leaves washing well. Sprinkle with salt and allow to stand.
2 Cut the green onions into thin strips. Chop the garlic and ginger finely.
3 Take two small green onions at

1 Trim and remove the outer leaves from the radish. Sprinkle them well with salt and let them stand.

Ingredients 10 Korean white radishes, 1 bundle small green onion, 1 firm Korean pear, 20 green thin Korean peppers, 5 red peppers, ¼ lb. ginger, 5 cloves garlic, 3 cups coarse salt, water

Method **1** Select small, firm radishes. Remove the fine roots. Wash and drain.
2 Wash and tie the green onions together five at a time making bundles.
3 Slice the ginger and garlic thinly. Wrap the slices in gauze and tie.
4 Roll the radishes in salt. Place the radishes, **#3** ginger-garlic peeled pear and green peppers in

1 Roll the radishes in salt.

2 Tie the small green onions into bundles of 5 each.

3 Wrap the garlic and ginger slices in gauze and tie.

a time and make them into a small bundle.

4 When the radish is well-salted, wash it and drain to remove any excess water. Mix the salted radish with the red pepper powder until the color sets.

5 When the radish is deeply colored, add the chopped garlic, green onion, salt, salted anchovy juice, sugar and small green onion and mix thoroughly. Place the radish kimchi in a crock.

Hint   Select radishes with fresh green tops and thick, stubby roots.

2 First mix the radish with red pepper powder and then add the remaining ingredients and mix thoroughly.

a crock and sprinkle with salt.

5 Three days later, pour salt water into the crock.

6 Cover the top with the radish leaves and weigh them down with something heavy.

Hint   To store the vegetables in an underground pit, choose a dry place facing toward the south. Dig 2 meters deep, place the radish upside down, stack the carrots and put the cabbages in the middle. Cover and make a ventilating hole on the top.

4 Add enough salt water to cover the radishes.

Stuffed Cucumber Kimchi
Oisobagi (오이소박이)

Ingredients   3 cucumbers, 5 tbsp. salt, 2 green onions, 1 clove garlic, ¼ bundle small wild leeks, 1 round onion, 6 tbsp. red pepper powder, 1 tbsp. sugar, 1 tbsp. salted soused shrimp. 1 tsp. salt

Method   **1** Clean the cucumbers rubbing them with salt and cut them into 2⅓″ lengths. Cut long slits lengthwise through the cucumber, leaving the ends intact Sprinkle with salt and allow to stand for several hours.

1 Cut slits through the cucumbers, sprinkle them with salt and let them stand.

2 Chop the round onion , green onions and garlic. Cut the small leeks into ⅓″ lengths.

2 Chop the green onion, garlic and round onion finely. Cut the small leeks into ⅓″ lengths.

3 Grind the red pepper powder with hot water in a mortar. Add the shrimp juice, small leeks, chopped round onion, garlic, green onion, sugar and salt to the ground red pepper powder and mix well.

4 Dry off the excess water from the salted cucumbers. Stuff the slits with the **#3** mixture.

3 Grind the red pepper powder and salted soused shrimps with hot water. Add the **#2** vegetables and mix well.

4 Dry the excess water from the salted cucumbers and stuff the slits with the **#3** mixture.

Hot Radish Kimchi
Kkakttugi (각두기)

Dried Radish Strips in Soy Sauce
Muumallaengijangatchi (무우말랭이장아찌)

Ingredients 1 Korean white radish, ⅓ cup coarse salt, 2 cloves garlic, 1 knob ginger, 1 green onion, ½ cup red pepper powder, ¼ bundle watercress, 1 tbsp. sugar, 1 tsp. sesame seed, 1 tbsp. salted soused shrimp

Method 1 Select plump, firm Korean radish. Cut the radish into cubes ¾" ✕ 1". Sprinkle with salt and let stand.

2 Cut the green onion and water-

1 Cut the radish into cubes ¾" ✕ 1".

Ingredients ½ lb. dried Korean white radish strips, 2 cups soy sauce, 1 green onion, 1 clove garlic, 1 knob ginger, 2 tbsp. red pepper powder, 1 tsp. sesame salt, 3 tbsp. sugar, 1 tbsp. sesame oil, red pepper threads, MSG

Method 1 Soak the dried radish strips in water and clean them rubbing them between your hands. Squeeze out the water.

2 Sprinkle the radish cubes well with salt and mix them with the red pepper powder.

3 Add the glutinous rice paste-gruel, sugar, salted shrimps, garlic and ginger and mix well.

Dried Radish Strips in Soy Sauce

1 Soak the dried radish strips in water and clean them.

54

Cucumbers in Soy Sauce
Oijangatchi (오이장아찌)

cress stems into 2″ lengths.

3 Mix the salted radish cubes with the red pepper powder. Boil the glutinous rice flour with water into a thin paste-gruel and let cool.

4 Add the green onion, watercress, garlic, ginger and glutinous rice paste-gruel to the colored radish and mix well. Season with salt.

Soak them in soy sauce and allow them to stand overnight.

2 Add the sugar, sesame oil, chopped garlic, ginger, MSG, red pepper threads and sesame salt and mix well.

Ingredients   10 dark green seedless cucumbers, 1 cup coarse salt, 3 cups soy sauce, 3 tbsp. sugar, 1 green onion, 2 cloves garlic, 2 tsp. sesame oil, red pepper threads, 1 tsp. sesame seed

Method   **1** Select fresh, long cucumbers. Sprinkle the cucumbers with salt, weigh them down with a heavy stone and let them stand for 10 days.

1 Sprinkle the cucumbers with salt, weigh them down with a heavy stone and let them stand for 10 days.

2 Cut the cucumbers into thin sticks and soak them in cold water to remove the saltiness.

2 When the cucumbers are well-salted, cut them into thin sticks and rinse to remove the saltiness.

3 Simmer 3 cups soy sauce and 3 tbsp. sugar in a pot and cool.

4 Pour the **#3** liquid over the salted cucumbers and let them stand overnight.

5 Remove the **#4** liquid and mix the cucumbers with the remaining seasoning.

3 Simmer the soy sauce and sugar and let it cool. Pour the liquid over the cucumbers.

4 Remove the **#3** liquid and mix the cucumber with the seasonings.

2 Squeeze out the water and marinate them in soy sauce.

3 Mix the **#2** strips with the seasonings.

Sesame Leaves in Soy Sauce
Kkaennipchangatchi (깻잎장아찌)

Todok in Red Sauce
Tŏdŏkchangatchi (더덕장아찌)

Ingredients 200 sesame leaves, 1 tbsp. whole sesame seed, 1 head garlic, 1 cup soy sauce, 2 tbsp. sugar, red pepper threads, 1 red pepper, 2 tbsp. red pepper powder, 2 chestnuts, 1 knob ginger

Method **1** Select tender sesame leaves. Wash them well and pat dry with a cloth.
2 Cut the chestnuts and garlic into thin strips.
3 Mix the soy sauce, red pepper strips, chopped ginger, sesame seed, garlic, chestnuts, red pepper threads, sugar and red pepper power to make the seasoning sauce
4 Place the sesame leaves one on top of the other in a bowl and sprinkle them with the seasoning sauce. Sprinkle all the sesame leaves with the seasoning sauce. Place them in a jar and weigh them down with a heavy stone.

1 Wash the sesame leaves and pat off excess water.

2 Make the seasoning sauce with all the ingredients.

3 Sprinkle the sesame leaves with the seasoning sauce.

Ingredients ½ lb. todok (a white root), 1 cup red pepper paste, 2 green onions, 3 cloves garlic, 1 tbsp. sesame salt, 1 tbsp. sugar, 1 tsp. sesame oil

Method **1** Peel the todok and soak them in salt water to remove the bitterness. Pound the todok into flat, thin pieces with a round stick.
2 Dry excess water from the

Todok in Red Sauce

Sugared Seaweed
Miyŏkchaban (미역자반)

Ingredients 1 oz. brown seaweed, 2 tbsp. sugar, 4 tbsp. sesame oil, sesame seed

Method 1 Cut the seaweed into bite-sized pieces.

2 Heat the sesame oil in a fry pan and add the seaweed pieces a few at a time and fry just until crisp.

3 Drain the fried seaweed pieces on paper to remove the oil. Sprinkle with the sugar and sesame seed.

Hint This crispy seaweed (or fried tangle) may be crumbled onto hot boiled rice or stir-fried rice with vegetable.

2 Heat the sesame oil in a fry pan and fry the seaweed pieces.

1 Soak the todok in salt water to remove the bitterness.

2 Dry excess water from the todok and pound it with a round stick.

3 Mix the todok with the red pepper paste.

todok. Mix the dried todok with the red pepper paste and place it in a jar.

3 When the todok is deeply colored, take it out of the jar. Shred it finely and season it with the chopped green onion, sesame salt, sugar and sesame oil.

Hint Add well-fermented red pepper paste to the todok.

1 Cut the seaweed into bite-sized pieces.

3 Drain the fried seaweed pieces on paper and sprinkle with the sugar and sesame seed.

57

Deep-Fried Laver
Kimbugak (김부각)

Deep-Fried Sesame Leaves
Kkaennippugak (깻잎부각)

Ingredients 20 sheets laver, ½ cup glutinous rice powder, 1 cup glutinous rice, ¼ cup sesame seed, 1 tbsp. sugar, 1 tbsp. salt, salad oil

Method 1 Boil the glutinous rice powder with salt and water to

Ingredients 20 sesame leaves, ½ cup glutinous rice powder, ½ cup glutinous rice, 2 tbsp. sesame seed, salad oil, 1 tsp. sugar, 2 tsp. salt

Method 1 Select tender and well-formed sesame leaves. Clean well and pat off excess water.

make a thin paste-gruel. Spread the paste on each sheet of laver, stick two sheets together and dry them in the sun.

2 Lay half of the dried laver sheets flat and spread the paste on one side of the sheets again. Then

1 Put the glutinuous rice paste on each sheet of laver and stick two sheets together.

2 Boil the glutinous rice powder with salt and water to make a thin paste-gruel. Steam the glutinous rice, adding salt water, in a steamer.

3 Brush the paste-gruel on half of the dried sesame leaves and sprinkle with sesame seeds. Put the steamed glutinous rice on the

sprinkle them with the sesame seed and dry in the sun. Spread the rest of the dried laver sheets with boiled glutinous rice and dry on a wicker tray. Cut the dried sheets of laver into bite-sized pieces and deep-fry in oil at 320°F.

2 Spread boiled glutinous rice on each sheet of laver, dry and deep-fry them.

rest of the sesame leaves. Place all the sesame leaves on a wicker tray and dry them in the sun.

4 Deep-fry them until crisp in oil at 360°F.

5 Sprinkle the deep-fried sesame leaves with salt and sugar while still hot.

Deep-Fried Laver

Deep-Fried Sesame Leaves

Salted and Spiced Oysters
Ŏriguljŏt (어리굴젓)

Salted Roe of Pollack
Myŏngnanjŏt (명란젓)

Ingredients 1 lb. oysters, 4 tbsp. salt, ⅔ cup red pepper powder, 1 tbsp. sugar, 1 clove garlic, 1 knob ginger

Method 1 Wash the oysters in salt water and drain. Sprinkle the oysters with salt and let them stand for 2-3 days in a cool place.

2 Season the oysters with the red pepper powder, sugar, garlic and ginger. Place the seasoned oysters in a jar and store in cool place.

1 Wash the oysters in salt water and drain.

2 Season the oysters with the red pepper powder, sugar, garlic and ginger.

1 Brush the glutinous rice paste-gruel on the sesame leaves.

2 Sprinkle the sesame leaves with the sesame seed, dry and deep-fry.

Ingredients ⅔ lb. roe of pollack, ½ cup red pepper powder, ½ cup salt, 2 heads garlic, 3 knobs ginger, sesame seed

Method 1 Sprinkle the roe of pollack with salt and let it stand overnight.

2 Place layer upon layer of the roe in a jar adding the red pepper powder, chopped garlic, ginger and salt. Cover the top with vinyl and press it with a heavy weight. Three weeks later, sprinkle with the sesame oil and sesame seed and serve.

Salted Roe of Pollack

Pickled Crabs
Kejŏt (게젓)

Pickled Squids
Kkolttugijŏt (꼴뚜기젓)

1 Remove the shells from the crabs, clean them and cut them into pieces.

Ingredients   3 red crabs, 1 tbsp. sugar, 2 cups soy sauce, 3 cloves garlic, 1 knob ginger, 1 tsp. sesame oil, red pepper threads, 1 tsp. sesame seed, 2 tbsp. salt

Method   **1** Wash fresh crabs and remove the shells. Cut them into pieces and sprinkle them with salt.
2 Mix the soy sauce with the garlic, red pepper threads, ses-

Ingredients   ½ lb squid, 6 tbsp. red pepper powder, 2 tbsp. sugar, 1 tbsp. corn syrup, 5 cloves garlic, 1 knob ginger, MSG, 1 tsp. sesame oil, 1 tsp. sesame seed, ½ white Korean radish, 1 red pepper

Method   **1** Remove the skin and the entrails from the salted squid. Cut them into thin strips and rinse them in cold water twice.

2 Mix the red pepper powder, chopped ginger, sugar, grain syrup, garlic, sesame salt and MSG to make the seasoning sauce.
3 Add the seasoning sauce to the squid and mix well. Then add sliced radish, red pepper and sesame oil and mix well.

1 Remove the skin and the entrails from the squid and cut into thin strips.

2 Add the seasoning sauce to the squid and mix well.

Pickled Squids

Salted Pollack Guts

60

Salted Pollack Guts
Ch'angnanjŏt (창란젓)

Salted Sole
Kajamishik'ae (가자미식해)

2 Pour the seasoning sauce over the crab pieces.

ame seed, ginger, MSG, sugar and sesame oil to make the seasoning sauce. Pour the seasoning sauce over the crab pieces, mix well and let them stand two hours before serving.

Hint One must eat the pickled crabs within a few days. For longer storage boil the soy sauce, cool it and pour it over the pickled crabs.

1 Cut the sole into pieces and sprinkle them with salt.

Ingredients 2 lb. guts (intestine) of walleye pollack, 1 cup red pepper powder, 2 heads garlic, 4 knobs ginger, 2 cups salt

Method **1** Clean the fresh fish guts. Wrap them in a cloth, weigh them down with a heavy stone and let stand overnight.
2 Sprinkle the well-dried guts with salt and allow them to stand overnight again.
3 Mix the salted guts with the chopped garlic, ginger and red pepper powder. Place the mixture in a jar and let stand for 15 days before serving.

Hint About 15 days later, take a little guts out of the jar, mix it with salted radish, garlic and red pepper powder and let it stand for 3-4 days before serving.

Ingredients 10 sole, 2 cups hulled millet, 2 cups salt, 2 heads garlic, 2 cups red pepper powder, 1 white Korean radish, 2 oz ginger

Method **1** Select small fresh sole. Scale the fish, remove the entrails, clean them and dry off excess water. Cut them into pieces and leave them under salt for 2 days. When the surface of the sole gets hard, drain them on a wicker basket. Boil the hulled millet leaving it a little bit hard; cool.
2 Mix the sole pieces with the

2 Mix the boiled hulled millet with the red pepper powder, ginger and chopped garlic.

3 Combine the **#1**, **#2** ingredients working in red pepper powder by hand.

boiled millet, garlic and red pepper powder. Place the mixture in a jar, cover the top with vinyl and weigh it down with something heavy.
3 When the sole ripens (two weeks later), cut the radish into thick strips, sprinkle it with salt and squeeze it tightly.
4 Mix the sole pieces with the radish strips, garlic, ginger and red pepper powder and check the seasoning. Place the mixture in a jar and seal.

4 Place the **#3** mixture in a jar and cover the top with vinyl. Weigh it down and let it stand for two weeks.

5 When the **#4** sole ripens, add the radish and mix well.

Fermented Soybean Lumps
Meju (메주)

Soy Sauce
Kanjang (간장)

Soy Sauce

Ingredients   18 lb. dried yellow soybeans
Method   **1** Wash the soybeans and soak them in water overnight; drain.

2 Boil the soybeans in water on high heat. When they come to a boil, reduce the heat and simmer until the soybeans are thoroughly cooked. Drain the soybeans and pound them to a fine pulp while

1 Boil the soybeans thoroughly, drain well and pound them to a fine pulp while still hot.

Ingredients   2 fermented soybean lumps (9 lb.), 12 cups coarse salt, 30 liter water, 3 pieces of charcoal, 3 dried red peppers, 5 jujubes, 1 tbsp. sesame seed

Method   **1** Remove the mold and the dust from the fermented soybean lumps two days before using. Wash them and dry them well in the sun.

2 Prepare a clean earthenware crock. Put the 12 cups of salt on a wicker basket and pour the water over it to make salt water. Let it stand overnight, so that any dregs settle to the bottom.

3 Put layer on layer of the soybean lumps in the crock and pour the strained salt water through a fine sieve into the crock.

4 Float the jujubes, dried red peppers and burned charcoal in the

1 Brush away the mold from the soybean lumps and wash.

2 Dry the soybean lumps in the sun.

3 Dissolve the salt in water and strain it through a fine sieve.

62

hot in a mortar.

3 Shape the soybean pulp into square lumps tamping it tightly; dry them in the sun.

4 Put them in a box placing straw between the lumps so they do not stick together. Seal the box and allow the lumps to ferment.

5 When the soybean lumps are covered with white mold, dry them well and store them in a bag.

2 Shape the pounded soybeans into square lumps tamping it tightly.

crock and sprinkle the salt on the top. Then seal the crock with gauze and allow it to stand covered for a few days.

5 After 3 days whenever the sun shines, open the lid to expose the contents to the sun; cover at night.

6 After about 40 days, carefully take the soybean lumps out of the crock and place them into another crock.

7 Strain the soy sauce through a fine sieve and pour it into a crock allowing the dregs to settle to the bottom.

8 Boil the soy sauce in a large pot skimming the froth from the top. Then simmer the soy sauce a long time.

9 Let the boiled soy sauce cool and pour it in the crock again. Expose it to the sun on shiny days.

Ingredients   2 fermented soybean lumps (9 lb.), 1 cup coarse salt, 3 cups powdered red pepper seed

Method   **1** Mash the fermented soybean lumps which were left from making the soy sauce. Mix them with the powdered red pep-

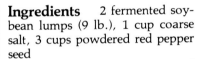

1 Add the salt to the mashed fermented soybeans and mix well.

per seed and salt.

2 Pack the **#1** mixture tightly in another crock. Sprinkle the top with quite a bit of salt.

Hint   Add some fermented soybean powder to the mashed soybean lumps and mix well for extra sweetness and nutrition.

2 Pack the **#1** mixture tightly in a crock.

3 Sprinkle the top with quite a bit of salt.

4 Place the soybean lumps into the crock and pour **#3** over them.

5 Add the jujubes, dried red peppers, charcoal and salt.

6 Skim the froth from the soy sauce and simmer.

Red Pepper Paste
Koch'ujang (고추장)

Ingredients 2 lb. fermented soybean powder, 6 lb. glutinous rice powder, 4 lb. red pepper powder, 5 cups malt, 6 cups coarse salt
Method 1 Dissolve the malt in hot water and strain it through a fine sieve. Mix the malt water with the glutinous rice powder and stir well.

2 Boil the #1 mixture on low heat to make a paste until golden brown and translucent; let it cool. If the paste is only half-boiled, it is apt to go bad.
3 Mix the paste first with the fermented soybean powder and stir well. Then add the red pepper powder and salt and stir well.

Place the mixture in the crock and sprinkle quite a bit of salt on the top. Seal the top with gauze and expose it to the sun.
Hint Break the half-fermented soybeans into small pieces and dry them in the sun. Pound them into powder and dry. This may be used to make the red pepper paste.

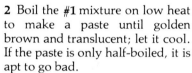

4 Cool the paste and add the fermented soybean powder.

6 Season the #5 mixture with salt and stir well.

1 Dissolve the malt in hot water and strain it through a fine sieve.

5 Add the red pepper powder to #4 and stir well.

7 Place the red pepper paste in a crock and sprinkle salt on the top.

2 Add the glutinous rice powder to the malt water and stir well.

3 Boil the #2 mixture on low heat until the paste becomes golden brown and translucent.

Dinner Table Setting

Pansang (반상)

"Pansang" means a Korean table-set for a dinner. There are 3-chop, 5-chop, 7-chop and 12-chop settings according to the number of the side dishes. A 7-chop table includes seven side dishes along with boiled rice, soup, three seasoning sauces, and two heavy soups. On the table above, the hot radish kimchi can be replaced with vegetable salad, and one of the heavy soups with raw meat.

Menu: boiled rice, soup, soy sauce, vinegar-red pepper paste, kimchi, hot radish kimchi, hot pollack soup, rib stew, broiled beef patties, skewered beef and vegetables, boiled mussel, mung bean pancakes, seasoned cucumber with vinegar, and broiled fish.

Baby's First Birthday Table
Tolsang (돌상)

The "Tolsang" setting for celebrating baby's first birthday can be varied according to one's family circumstances and taste. This table includes not only food but also a writing brush, inkstone, book, cotton thread, money and archery bow, symbols used to wish the baby success, longevity and a happy future. This custom has been handed down from generation to generation.

Menu: noodles, stuffed jujubes, sweet glutinous rice cakes, steamed rice cake, half-moon-shaped rice cake, fruits, cookies, millet dumplings, glutinous rice cake coated with bean flour, and rice.

Bride's Gift Table
P'yebaeksang (폐백상)

"P'yebaek" is a procedure wherein the bride makes a deep bow and offers her gifts to her parents-in-law. This custom is somewhat different according to the province and one's family. However, when the bride makes a deep bow to her parents-in-law, they throw jujubes in her skirt, wishing their descendants prosperity and good luck. The P'yebaek table is necessary for this formality.

How to wrap P'yebaek gifts in kerchieves: Make red and blue tasseled square kerchieves. Place the P'yebaek gifts on the tasseled kerchieves. Don't tie, but hold up, four edges of the kerchief together and fasten with a bond of white paper. Menu: stuffed jujubes, broiled beef patties, chestnuts, nine section dish of delicacies, wine, chicken.

New Year's Day Table
Sŏlsang (설상)

The first day in January is New Year's Day. Since early times Koreans wear gala dress and perform memorial rites for ancestors and make a round of New Year's calls to elder members of the family and community. This table for guests is set and served with wholeheartedly buoyed up by hopes for the New Year.

Menu: rice cake dumplings, cookies, sesame cookies, sweet rice dish, sweet rice drink, skewered beef and vegetables, mung bean pancakes, steamed shrimp, fried rice cake, kimchi, hot radish kimchi, glutinous rice cake, boiled pork, nine section dish, red snapper casserole, broiled beef patties, wrapped-up kimchi, jujube balls, chestnut balls, water-kimchi, whole cabbage kimchi, coated sweet rice cakes, steamed shank of beef, soy sauce, vinegar-soy sauce, and rice wine.

Drinking Table
Chuansang (주안상)

The "Chuansang" table is set for appetizers served with drinks.
The side-dishes can be varied according to the kinds of drinks.
Prepare several special side dishes such as fried food, meat
jerky, boiled pressed meats, hot stew and vegetable salad.
Menu: dried side dishes, steamed lobster, mung bean pancake,
skewered food, boiled pork, and wine.

GLOSSARY

Angelica Shoots (turūp) are young shoots with tender green leaves of the angelica bush which are available fresh only in early spring.

Bamboo Shoots (chuksun) are the tender spring sprouts of the bamboo, off-white in color and shaped like a bud. Their flesh is tender but firm and should be scalded about 5 minutes in boiling water if used fresh.

Barley Tea (porich'a) is tea made from toasted barley kernels. It is prepared by adding the toasted barley to boiling water, boiling for 5 minutes, straining and serving. Barley tea is served cooled in the summer and warm in the winter. Corn tea is prepared and served the same way but is made from parched corn kernels.

Bean Curd (tubu) is a square or rectangular cake of pressed, coagulated soybean puree—the "cheese" of soymilk. It has a bland texture and is a very easy-to-digest, nutritious food. It should be kept in water (changing water daily) in the refrigerator.

Beans: There are a large variety of dried beans available in the Korean grain-bean shops. In addition there are various processed bean foods also available for daily use in the Korean diet.

— yellow soybeans (hūink'ong), sprouts (k'ongnamul), bean curd (tubu), soft bean curd (sundubu), bean paste (toenjang), fermented soybeans for making soy sauce (meju), seasoned fermented soybeans (ch'ōnggukchang), soybean flour (k'ongkaru), soy sauce (kanjang).

— Brown soybeans (pamk'ong—literally "chestnut beans") are a chestnut brown color and have a smooth chestnut-like texture when cooked.

— Black soybeans (kŏmūnk'ong) are served as a side dish.

— mung beans (noktu), sprouts (sukchu namul), jellied mung bean puree (ch'ŏngp'o), mung bean flour (noktu karu).

— red kidney beans (kangnamk'ong)

Bean Sprouts (k'ongnamul) may be grown at home, if desired, in a warm, wet jar or purchased in most vegetable sections of grocery stores. The large sprouts are from the yellow soybean; the smaller more delicate sprouts are from the green mung bean.

Bellflower Root (toraji) is a white root from the mountainside bellflower.

Bracken (kosari) is the early spring shoot of the fern plant. These shoots are gathered in the spring and sold fresh at that time. They are also dried for re-hydration later in the year. There is a common variety and a rather special royal fern variety that has larger, softer shoots.

Burdock Root (uong) is a long, fat nutritious root with a distinctive flavor which is washed, scrubbed and scraped, soaked in vinegar-water so that it does not change color and then cut into thick strips for use.

Chinese Cabbage (paech'u) is a solid, oblong head of wide stalk-leaves with a subtle flavor used widely in making kimchi.

Chinese Noodles (tangmyōn) are very thin transparent noodles made from mung bean flour. They are sold dried in long loops. They should be soaked in warm water before use and cooked quickly. When cooked they become opaque and slippery.

Cinnamon (kyep'i) is a rough brown bark. It can be used whole or dried and ground to use in seasoning.

Eggplant (kaji) is the long, purple, shiny fruit of the eggplant plant; it is not large and round but sleek and elongated with a slight bulbousness at the end opposite the stem.

Garland Chrysanthemum (ssukkat) is a pungent, edible variety of Chrysanthemum; the leaves are used for seasoning and decorating like lettuce leaves in Korean recipes.

Garlic (manūl), related to the onion, has a bulb made up of several cloves with a strong odor and flavor. It is widely used as seasoning in Korean dishes after being finely chopped. Garlic is also served pickled and its long green stems are eaten raw or boiled.

Ginger Root (saenggang) adds zip to many Korean dishes. Fresh ginger root has a thin light-brown skin over knobby bulbs. It may be washed and dried and placed in the freezer in a plastic bag. It is then available for grating into whatever dish is being prepared. It may be dried and powdered but fresh ginger is called for in most Korean recipes.

Gingko Nuts (ūnhaeng) are oval-shaped, yellowish nuts with a soft texture. The shelled nuts may be stir-fried until green after which the outer skin will peel off easily. The peeled nuts are used for garnish on many special Korean dishes.

Ginseng (insam) is a much-prized root cultivated in Korea and China. This perennial herb is used mostly for medicinal purposes and is widely acclaimed for its rejuvenating qualities. It is usually sold dried, but fresh roots and rootlets are used in cooking. Ginseng tea and wine are popular in Korea.

Glutinous Rice (ch'apsal) is a white rice with a sticky consistency when cooked.

Glutinous Rice Flour (ch'apsal karu) is the flour from glutinous rice which is used in making Korean rice cakes.

Grain Syrup (choch'ŏng) is similar to dark corn syrup and is used as a sweetener. It is made by boiling "yot," a Korean candy base, with water and sugar until thick. Honey or sugar syrup can be used instead of this grain syrup in most recipes.

Green Onions: There are many varieties of green onions in Korea.

— (ch'ŏngp'a)—a medium sized variety harvested in the spring

— (puch'u)—a small, wild leek with a pungent flavor

— (shilp'a)—a thread-like onion with a taste similar to but stronger than chives

— (tallae)—a small, wild onion from the mountain meadows

Green Peppers, Korean (p'utkoch'u), are long, narrow unripe chili peppers and are usually hot to taste.

Indian Mustard Leaf (kat) is a green leaf available spring and autumn; Japanese "haruna."

Jujubes (taech'u) are similar to a date, usually used dried, for cooking or medicinal purposes. They should be soaked before using.

Kimchi is a spicy, slightly fermented pickle like vegetable dish accompanying every Korean meal. It is made from Chinese cabbage, Korean white radish, cucumber or other seasonal vegetables which are wilted with salt, stuffed with seasoning such as red pepper powder, chopped garlic, ginger juice and soused salted shrimp juice and fermented in earthenware crocks.

Konyak is jellied potato puree; it is sliced and used somewhat like a noodle.

Laver (kim) is cultivated carefully in the seabeds offshore in Korea and is of excellent quality. It is sold in packages of folded paper-thin sheets. It is used for wrapping rice rolls or broiled to a delicate crispness and served with a rice meal.

Lotus Root (yŏn-gūn) is the root of the lotus flower. It is grey on the outside but when cut open a beautiful lacy effect is formed in each slice by several open tubes which run the length of the root. It is served as a vegetable or candied as a sweet.

Malt Powder (yŏtkirūm) is dried sprouted barley which has been crushed into a powder. It is used to aid fermentation in making wines and drinks; it is a good food for yeast.

Mushrooms: There are several varieties used both fresh and dried.

— Brown oak mushrooms (p'yogo) (Japanese shiitake) are used in meat dishes after soaking well in warm water.

— Stone mushrooms (sŏgi) also should be soaked before using.

— Jew's ear mushrooms (mogi) are large, delicate ear-shaped fungi.

— Pine mushrooms (songi) grow on pine tree trunks; they are most often sold fresh or canned; very tasty when sliced and sauteed.

Pear, Korean (pae) is a crisp, large, round, firm, sweet, apple-like pear which is very juicy. It has a tan outside skin and a cream-colored flesh with dark brown seeds. Harvested in the fall it keeps well in rice-hulls in a cool place. It is considered to be an aid in digestion.

Pine Nut (chat) is the nut-like edible, soft-textured, somewhat oily seeds of the pinon tree. They are used to make a gruel-soup and in garnishing drinks and other foods.

Pine Nut Powder is ground or finely chopped pine nuts used for rolling sweet rice cakes and other delicacies.

Pulgogi is Korea's best-known charcoal-broiled marinated beef dish. It is traditionally broiled over charcoal in a slotted pan but it may be oven-broiled or quickly pan-broiled.

Radish, Korean White (muu) is a round, long, firm white root much larger than a red or white table radish. The taste is sweet when first harvested and its texture is crisp and juicy. It is a basic kimchi ingredient; it is sometimes dried for making soups in the winter and small, young radishes are used for a special spring kimchi.

Red Pepper Paste (koch'ujang) is a dark reddish paste made from fermented soybean and red pepper powder mixed with glutinous rice flour and malt. It is spicy hot and widely used to thicken and season soups and stews. It will keep well in the refrigerator.

Red Peppers (koch'u) are a basic Korean seasoning ingredient. They are small, long peppers similar to cayenne and are hot to the taste. They are dried and ground or cut into threads or used fresh for seasoning or garnish. They are very high in vitamin A.

Rice Cake (ttŏk) is a delicacy served at most celebrations in Korea. It is made by steaming a glutinous rice flour dough which has been filled or mixed with various foods such as sesame seed, beans, mugwort, nuts, jujube, raisins; the dough is usually shaped beautifully into half-moons, circles or other soft shapes.

Rice Wine (ch'ŏngju) is a clear white wine made from rice used for drinking and cooking.

Salted Soused Shrimp (saeujŏt) are tiny shrimp which have been salted and become somewhat pickled and juicy; used in making kimchi and in seasoning.

Sesame Leaves (kkaennip) are the beautifully shaped pungent leaves of the sesame plant which are served as a vegetable in a sauce or deep-batter-fried.

Sesame Oil (ch'amgirūm) is pressed from toasted sesame seeds. It has a unique flavor and only a little is needed to add an authentic taste to Korean dishes.

Sesame Salt (kkaesogūm) is a mixture of toasted, crushed sesame seeds and salt. Add 1 teaspoon of salt to each cup of seeds. It is a basic Korean seasoning.

Sesame Seeds: White (hūinkkae), black (kōmūnkkae) and round brown (tūlkkae) are all used in Korean seasoning and in Korean candy-cookies.

Shinsollo is the name of a one-dish meal which is cooked at the table in a brass brazier "hot pot" which holds the charcoal in the center allowing the food to cook around it in a well-seasoned broth. It is a special occasion dish requiring hours of preserving preparation so that each food is cut precisely to the right shape and partially pre-cooked to allow for just the right last minute cooking at the table.

Soybean Paste (toenjang) is a thick brown paste made from a mixture of mashed fermented soybean lumps (left from making the soy sauce), powdered red pepper seeds and salt. It is used as a thickener for soups and stews and will keep well in the refrigerator.

Soy Sauce (kanjang) is a brownish-black salty liquid made by cooking fermented soybean cakes with water and salt. Each household in Korea used to make their own soy sauce in the spring; some still do. These are mild and add good flavor to most any food. Soy sauce is used in cooking, especially meats, but is also placed on the table to use as a dip for sauteed vegetables, fish and meat. The Japanese soy sauce is less salty but sweeter than Korean soy sauce.

Sweet Red Beans (p'at) are small and round and used widely in Korean confections. When cooked and mashed they are sweet and soft-textured. This sweet bean puree is used as filling in rice cakes and also now in donuts and rolls.

Todok is a fibrous white root found in the mountain in the spring. It must be pounded with a mallet and washed with salty water to take away its puckery taste before seasoning and cooking. It is an appetite stimulant.

Watercress (minari) is an aromatic plant used frequently in Korean cooking, especially the stems. It is not exactly the same as watercress but almost. The delicate leaves may be added to soups and are good with fish.

Most, if not all, of these ingredients may be purchased in Oriental groceries.

INDEX

INDEX OF KOREAN RECIPE TITLES